WOMEN
...NEGLECTED MAJORITY OR MONSTROUS REGIMENT?

DAYS OF DECISION

Series Editor: Julia Neuberger

WOMEN

...NEGLECTED MAJORITY OR MONSTROUS REGIMENT?

PAPERMAC

First published 1987 by
PAPERMAC
a division of Macmillan Publishers Limited
4 Little Essex Street London WC2R 3LF
and Basingstoke
Associated companies in Auckland, Delhi, Dublin, Gaborone,
Hamburg, Harare, Hong Kong, Johannesburg, Kuala Lumpur,
Lagos, Manzini, Melbourne, Mexico City, Nairobi, New York,
Singapore, and Tokyo

British Library Cataloguing in Publication Data
Neuberger, Julia
    Women: neglected majority or monstrous regiment?——(Days of decision).——
    (Papermac)
    1. Women——Great Britain——Social
    conditions
    I. Title.   II. Baker, Mary   III. Ewart-Biggs, Jane   IV. Stott, Mary
    V. Series
    305.4'2'0941   HQ1593

ISBN 0-333-44769-7

Typeset by Columns of Reading
Printed by Richard Clay plc, Bungay, Suffolk

Contents

Introduction

Sexual politics has been one of the key issues of the late twentieth century. All political parties now pay attention to 'women's issues', and the women's vote is sought across the political spectrum. Yet the economic position of women in the workforce in relation to men is now getting worse, and the protective legislation designed to help them is full of holes, or inadequately applied.

All three contributors are conscious of the problem, but approach it from a very different perspective from that of the 'radical' feminists of the 1960s – partly because of a growing awareness that 1960s and 1970s legislation did not provide all the answers, and partly out of an increasing concern for families in poverty, many of which are headed by women. All three emphasise that most women's lives are played out in a family setting, and it is the problems and difficulties of that environment that particularly need addressing. At the same time they see possibilities for increasing respect for women and for expanding women's horizons by encouraging them to be more active in public life, and campaigning for men to put women into top positions in companies, quangos, and charities.

Seventy years after the Suffragettes, twenty-five years after the beginning of 'women's lib', and eight years after a woman became Prime Minister for the first time, women's policy has clearly become a crucial election issue again.

Julia Neuberger

Opening Doors for Women

Mary Baker

Enormous changes have taken place in women's lives during this century – many because of advances in medicine such as birth control, many because new household appliances have reduced the time and drudgery of housework, and many because of long campaigns by women for equal and just treatment, campaigns which have led to votes for all women over 21 (now 18) with the Equal Franchise Act of 1928, the Equal Pay Act of 1970, and the Sex Discrimination Act of 1975.

Conservatives believe in choice, and their view of the importance of the individual within the law underlies the Conservative Party's commitment to equal opportunities for women. We believe in open doors; many that were once barred to women are now plainly open, but some, though unlocked, still need a good shove to demonstrate to our daughters that women do have a vast range of futures waiting for them. Indeed you can say that women have a potentially greater range than men, for one of our commitments is to ensure that those doors marked 'Home Management' and 'Childcare' stay open to all – men as well as women – as important options in our choices for life. Too often nowadays these options are made to look less significant, and the skills required less praiseworthy, than the high-earning lifestyles of big city business.

Two articles in a recent edition of *Cosmopolitan* magazine make the point. One, about Fiona Halton who ran the immensely successful British Film Year, is headed 'Work is Heaven'. On the same page the former Deputy Editor of *Cosmopolitan*, Pat Garrett, talks about her feelings on becoming a mother: 'Emotionally I feel a millionaire – with access to one of the most exclusive clubs in the world: motherhood.'

The keys that we've used to open doors, and the doors that still need oiling, come up in my next two chapters. They demonstrate the continuing necessity for policies for women and, perhaps even more, for policies for families – parents of young children, adults with ageing relatives.

It's not a question of throwing buns through the bars to keep women happy. Only when all the barriers are down can men and women play a full and equal part, with mutual respect and support, at work, in the community, and in the home.

I was brought up in Scotland with three brothers and the unspoken expectation that we all shared the work that had to be done indoors and out; that we would all take education seriously; and that if required we could all cook, all reef a mainsail, and all clean fish and sparking-plugs. During the war there weren't too many men about, but Scotswomen have been used to similar situations in their history and I remember my father as always a friend, a teacher and storyteller, and a great if occasional cook. I didn't begin to think about 'equality', except in the sense that Robert Burns wrote about it, until I came south in my twenties.

Women in the Conservative Party and Their Involvement in Policy-Making

For over eighty years Conservative women have organised themselves to support their party, to ensure their influence was positive and effective, and to establish communication lines up to Parliament, and back through the Areas to women in the constituencies.

Today there must be well over a million women in Britain who subscribe to the Conservative Party, quite apart from the many more who vote Conservative at elections. Conservative women lead the way in organising themselves to participate actively in the political process as a powerful group.

One of the earliest mentions of a formal movement was in 1904 when twenty-six women's branches turned out to support the Conservative candidate at a by-election in Oswestry. In 1918 the rules of the National Union Association were amended to provide for the inclusion of women in the party organisation, and the Chairman, Vice-Chairman and three members of the Women's Unionist Association were invited to serve on the party's National Executive Committee.

The real turning point came with the end of the First World War. 'After the very big part they had played in the war effort,' recalled the former MP Lady Davidson, 'women were hungry for political activity.'

In 1926 the first woman to be elected Chairman of a political party was Dame Caroline Bridgeman. Since then there have been many more women who have chaired the National Union and who come into the public eye via television when they are seen chairing the annual party conference.

In 1920 the first Annual Conservative Women's Conference was held. Within five years attendance had rocketed from just under 400 in 1920 to 2314 in 1924. The huge demand for seats took even the organisers by surprise as 1600 women from 304 constituencies besieged the hall. In 1928 the Conference Chairman announced: 'I am proud to say that the Women's Unionist Organisation in England and Wales has a membership of nearly a million.'

Contrary to what might have been expected, discussions were not solely concerned with 'women's subjects'. As today, women were determined to tackle the broader issues. The 1921 conference included such topics as 'Industrial Unrest' and 'How to Attract Young People'. The women found an enthusiastic champion in Lord Davidson who did not confine himself to paying the traditional tributes to 'incalculable service', but took positive action as Chairman of the party organisation from 1926–1930 to bring women more into the mainstream. The National Union rules were amended to make it a requirement that between a third and a half of the Executive Committee be women, and in 1928 the Central

Women's Advisory Committee was officially recognised and accorded much the same status as the Conservative Women's National Committee enjoys today.

In 1949 the first of a long series of booklets designed to stimulate discussion and advance ideas for reform was produced by the women of the party for the Annual Women's Conference. Called 'A True Balance' it advocated widespread changes for women, including equal rates of pay, the removal of discrimination against women peers, and the statutory right to transfer a tenancy to a single-parent mother with care of the children.

In 1968 Edward Heath set up the Cripps Committee to examine the legal position of women and to recommend changes to enable them to participate socially, economically and politically on an equal basis with men. Their report had a major impact and led, among other reforms, to the 1970 Equal Pay Act, the 1970 Criminal Justice Act making more women eligible for jury service, and the Guardianship Act 1973, giving equal rights for the guardianship of children to both parents. It also led to an important new measure in the 1972 Finance Act – the right for married women to elect to be taxed separately from their husbands. In 1973 the Conservative Government produced the consultative document 'Equal Opportunities for Men and Women' which proposed a whole raft of measures to end discrimination against women in the field of employment. It led to the setting up of the Equal Opportunities Commission and formed the basis of the 1975 Sex Discrimination Act which, with the Equal Pay Act, revolutionised women's career prospects.

Sara Morrison, Janet Young and currently Emma Nicholson have been distinguished Vice-Chairmen of the Conservative Party with special responsibility for the Women's Organisation. The current chairman reports regularly directly to the Prime Minister on the work and views of the women in the party.

International Women's Year, established by the United Nations in 1975, was marked in Britain by the election of Mrs Margaret Thatcher as party leader. The double impact of this remarkable person and the start of a decade of concentration on 'the maximum participation of women in all fields' has been very significant. While legislation changes behaviour, and ultimately can change attitudes, the process is vastly speeded up by a continually visible and powerful message.

In the 1970s the Conservative Women's National Committee (CWNC) became more involved in day to day politics, more professional, more confident about its role and its ability to influence government thinking. The rules were changed to encourage a broader representation on the committee and very real efforts were made to ensure that younger women were represented at branch and national level. Working parties were set up and pamphlets such as 'Work for Married Women' received much publicity. Many of the recommendations advocated in these publications were already on the statute book by the time the Conservatives left office in 1974. A large share of the credit for many of the reforms that have helped women belongs to the CWNC. Without their demand for action, and the research that went with it, legislation would certainly have taken much longer to become a reality.

The format of the Women's Conference has altered over the years. From a relatively staid affair, it has become a lively forum for genuine discussion. The new generation of women activists in the Conservative Party, with a formidable breadth of knowledge and experience, presents a vastly different picture from the caricature of 'Tory Ladies' in flowery hats beloved of cartoonists. Not only do they have expertise in home and family matters, but many are engaged in running small businesses, are employed in industry, have a profession or do valuable work in the community.

The work on policy that the Women's Organisation has been involved in in recent years includes regular proposals submitted to the Chancellor, pressing for example for the maintenance of the value of child benefit and for its payment direct to the caring parent, for the invalid care allowance to be made available to married women, and for greater recognition of part-time work.

Within the structure of the organisation, women in the constituencies meet and discuss subjects of current national and local concern which are then debated at Area level. Area Women's Organisations frequently produce study papers for the annual conference. In 1984, for example, the Eastern Area made a comparative study of women in public and political life in Britain and the other EEC countries. Wessex studied community amenities, and Wales the impact of new technology.

The chairmen of these regional areas, as well as the chairmen of the Scottish and Northern Ireland Women's Committees sit on the national committee with other co-opted members, of whom I was one for several years. From here are set up the working parties and the national surveys which have such an influence on legislation and plans for legislation. Reform of the law on sexual offences, on local rates, on tax for married couples, on the Warnock Report and on financial provisions for maternity are some of the more recent subjects of review.

All this consultation and input of women's views is over and above the regular constituency and Area committees, on all of which women sit, and many of which are chaired by women.

People sometimes deplore the idea of women-only groups, but in the interests of common sense and justice they are going to go on being important for as long as I can see. From a practical point of view women out at work share many interests and learn from each other as they make progress in new fields, while the last thing a woman at home, perhaps in a rural area, may want is to give up an evening or a Saturday to attend a meeting she could easily get to on a Tuesday morning.

Women who work unpaid in the home or in the local community may be closely and regularly in touch with a much wider range of people than those who sit in the same small office from nine to five each day. After all, one third of all women aged between sixteen and fifty-nine are not in paid work. That's well over five million women. Despite the significant annual increase in married women joining the labour force, 44 per cent of mothers with dependent children are not in paid work. Only 16.2 per cent of such mothers work full-time.

So many statements by political parties and pressure groups today forget or ignore women at home. But it is they above all who appreciate and use local services – buses, swimming pools, libraries, meals on wheels; they understand the significance of the changing patterns of small shops in the high street, or of the impact of environmental or broadcasting policies on those who may be elderly or handicapped or seeking work. Above all, they are the mothers who are taking a break from paid work to bring up their children themselves, working or studying part-time while their children are at school, or unable to return to appropriate work when their children finally leave school because their chosen role as homemaker over the years has lost them too much ground in the job market.

We value equally the views of all women in the Conservative Party. Over the last fifteen years far more meetings have been held at lunchtime, in the evenings or at weekends. The flexibility of the Conservative Women's Organisation is its great strength. Geared to the needs of women in widely differing circumstances, young and old, it enables all their views to be heard. Very often the many women who become local councillors or candidates for Parliament have cut their teeth in the supportive atmosphere of their local women's committee.

The new series of Highflyers conferences has brought together women in their twenties and thirties who have reached significant positions in their work, to meet, exchange ideas, and to discuss with government ministers the measures that concern them. Meetings such as these underline the pleasure and satisfaction of working with like-minded women, establish new networking possibilities, and make it possible for busy and successful younger women to input their views on policy directly.

The CWNC also works closely with Conservative women Members of Parliament and with the European Union of Women (EUW) – a union of women who are members of the centre and centre right political parties in Europe. It is the only organisation of its kind in existence and has consultative status with the Council of Europe and the United Nations Organisation. Its aims are close cooperation between women of like-minded political parties in Europe to exchange ideas, to discuss issues of social or political reform, to strengthen international understanding, and to encourage women to take a greater part in the decision-making processes of their own country. It was founded in 1955 in The Hague and now includes women of fourteen countries. Delegates from each member country attend a General Assembly every two years in a different host country. The British section of EUW has some 3000 members, many of whom participate in the international research commissions run by the organisation.

Areas of Special Interest to Women

Here I aim to cover seven separate areas where women may have special concerns – Childcare and Education, Social and Legal Provision for Families, Health and Safety, Women at Work, Tax, Women in the Community and Women of Influence. I will highlight the many changes that have already been made since the present Conservative Government came to power in 1979, and discuss further moves or changes that could be advantageous.

It's not designed as a polemic or an apologia; just a reasonable 'state of the art' report which might enable people to see what a Conservative programme can achieve for women; I think it also illustrates the difficulties of proposing that any one minister or department should have responsibility for policies for half the human race. Almost every field of action is seen to include areas of special relevance to women, and most of those naturally have an impact on men as well. The last thing I want is for men to feel that 'the women's side' is being looked after elsewhere and that they can concentrate on 'male issues', if there are such things.

Childcare and Education In 1985 47 per cent of all three- and four-year-olds were in nursery or primary schools, including the non-maintained sector.* This shows an increase from 35 per cent in 1976. Slightly over half the children were there for a full day. A similar number of under fives were in maintained or registered day nurseries, playgroups or with childminders; the great majority in registered playgroups.

Proper provision of good quality childcare is vital for mothers who work and for fathers with custody of their children. From the average child's point of view, from about two and a half or three years old, the half day which most nursery schools provide is probably sufficient stimulus for development.

The remarkable growth in part-time work for married women is a commercially apt response from industry to the needs of mothers and children. The development of the valuable Career-Break programmes for women in areas like banking and the civil service was pioneered by the Women's Medical Federation many years ago. These enable some women to take additional years off for childcare when their statutory maternity leave is up, and then to return to similar work without losing any grades or pension provision which has been built up. I strongly support such policies. In 1986, after extensive consultation with staff, Barclays Bank introduced a two-year full- or part-time Career-Break programme for women who had reached a certain level in the company. Thames Television is currently pursuing the establishment of a positive policy on part-timers and job-sharing to support their long-standing equal opportunities policy.

The Government itself, as an employer, is taking the lead with equal opportunities policies for women in the civil service, to maximise the potential of that most finite resource, people. In 1971 the first joint committee on equal opportunities for women in the civil service was set up, and in 1984

* *Social Trends* No. 17 (HMSO, 1987).

management and unions agreed on a joint programme of action.

Various schemes offering flexible work patterns have been introduced to make it possible for women – or men – to cope with domestic responsibilities and to continue their careers. When the Inland Revenue for example, introduced a formal part-time working agreement, within nine months almost five thousand of its staff (7 per cent) had chosen to work part-time. The Department of Health and Social Security (DHSS) have over 1000 job-sharers, and almost 2500 part-timers, including 70 men. Across the civil service some 170 staff at senior levels (Grade 7 and above) are also working part-time.

Two types of Career-Break programmes have been introduced in the civil service. In some departments a Keeping in Touch scheme offers people who resign for domestic reasons the chance to keep in touch and to be reinstated in preference to new recruits or promotees, if vacancies are available, for up to five years after resignation. One department also has a Commitment scheme which offers reinstatement to staff with high potential who agree to work for a short period each year during their absence.

Part-time work in senior clerical or junior management positions is a major innovation for companies to come to terms with, but it is vitally necessary if young women's talents and training are not to be wasted, and if their natural desire to choose to care for their young children without losing out on their future career is not to be thwarted.

The CWNC has recently expressed its concern that workplace nurseries, provided or supported by employers, have been taxed as a benefit in the hands of the parent, male or female, who uses them. For mothers who need or wish to work, the CWNC felt that such nurseries, where the mother can be easily in touch, and the hours coincide with her working hours, should not be discouraged.

At school the teacher–pupil ratio has improved from 18.9 to 1 in 1979 to 17.6 to 1 in 1985. In view of studies which have shown that teachers pay more attention to their boy pupils than to girls in class, perhaps the trend will now work in girls' favour. Work by Government on the development of a common core curriculum highlights the role it could play in a broader based curriculum. In particular the choices to be made at the age of fourteen would be limited, which in turn would help to reverse the tendency for girls to give up science and boys to give up languages around that age. Only 9.5 per cent of girl school-leavers in England passed physics 'O' level or the equivalent in 1985 (a 51 per cent improvement on the 1980 figures), compared with almost 22 per cent of boys leaving school. However, 28 per cent of girls leaving school passed maths 'O' level in 1985 compared with 33 per cent of boys.

In 1983 the Government established the Technical and Vocational Education Initiative (TVEI) which teaches work-related skills to fourteen- to eighteen-year-olds. Girls formed over 40 per cent of the participants in 1985. Over 90 per cent of them were studying a science, 40 per cent were on computer studies courses, and around 35 per cent were studying craft design and technology (CDT), well above the normal rates for girls studying these subjects. The study of CDT has been actively developed by the Conservative Government, and is involving many more girls in the design of products, and the handling of materials like wood, metal and plastic.

When the eleven plus exam was prevalent, girls regularly achieved higher marks than boys, although the boys' performance improved later on. However, girls are now beginning to maintain that early academic lead. A higher percentage of girls than boys regularly gain five or more 'O' levels at grades A to C, and in 1985 the percentage of girls with two or more 'A' levels (14.1 per cent) came close to that of boys (15.3 per cent).

Programmes like WISE (Women into Science and Engineering), set up by the Engineering Council and the Equal Opportunities Commission (EOC) and GIST (Girls into Science and Technology – a four-year project funded by the Economic and Social Research Council (ESRC), the Schools Council and the EOC to investigate why girls under-achieve in science and technology and to develop strategies for change in schools) aim to ensure that we use all the nation's talent productively. With a declining number of school-leavers it is imperative that girls as well as boys leave school trained in the skills for tomorrow's world.

Over half the students on non-advanced courses in colleges of further education are now women. Forty-eight per cent of students on advanced courses in polytechnics; and, in 1985, 42 per cent of university undergraduates were women, as well as 37 per cent of postgraduate students. Yet only around $2\frac{1}{2}$ per cent of university professors are women.

Rewriting established children's literature to remove references to what might nowadays be called sex-stereotyped behaviour does not accord with Conservative principles, but encouraging girls and boys to pursue all tasks and areas of educational achievement, and to ensure that no student is barred or discouraged from any subject because of their sex, certainly is at the heart of Conservative policy.

In 1980 a Department of Education and Science consultative paper on the curriculum suggested a greater emphasis on moral education and preparation for parenthood. Educating boys for responsible parenthood as well as girls, and teaching them the satisfactions as well as the responsibilities and the hard work involved in being a parent is something I strongly support.

In the Education Act of 1986 parents were granted more places on school governing bodies. This will take effect in 1988 when new elections for governing bodies will be held. The same Act gave governing bodies the right to decide on what, if any, type of sex education should be taught in their school. From September 1982 all parents were given the statutory right to express a preference for the school of their choice.

If all potential patients of the National Health Service were now refused the right to comment on or influence the Health Service, either in the press, or via their Community Health Council or Family Practitioner Committee, we'd be rightly amazed, although few of us would consider taking over the surgeon's job. In the same way, due consideration should be given to parents' views and beliefs about their children's education.

Many people now accept research that shows girls aged between eleven and sixteen may do better in single-sex schools. Some schools have been encouraged to experiment with physics or computer classes for girls only and are having encouraging results. The fact that the all-female body of undergraduates at an Oxford college recently voted to remain single sex shows that many girls and young women appreciate the value of a less sexually conscious environment as they approach maturity – somewhere where they can channel their ambitions along academic paths and keep the complicating factor of the opposite sex for after hours.

The Conservative Government strongly resisted moves by the EEC to challenge the right of the few remaining single-sex colleges at Oxford and Cambridge to appoint only women Fellows. An additional argument in favour of retaining this right is that as schools and colleges have moved to mixed operation, the opportunities for senior positions for women teaching staff have invariably declined. There are thus even fewer examples for girls and young women to emulate: the 'Role Models' of modern jargon.

Social and Legal Provisions for Families Child benefit, which replaced both the earlier child tax allowance and the cash benefit of family allowance, has remained as a key benefit to the family, tax free and payable direct to the caring parent, generally the mother. Over the years the Conservative Women's National Committee has regularly supported this benefit and the maintenance of its real value. Child benefit will continue to be paid to all families as at present.

Family income supplement (FIS) is based on gross income. The new Family Credit which will replace it in 1988 is based on net income (after tax and national insurance), and aims to provide help on a considerably larger scale to low-earning families working twenty-four hours or more per week. Forty per cent of all families who are on FIS are lone parents. The Government expects that about twice as many families will be helped by the new scheme as by FIS. It has now been agreed that Family Credit will go direct to the caring parent, and families on Family Credit will get extra cash instead of vouchers for school meals.

The new income support scheme will replace supplementary benefit in 1988. This aims to give increased support to all low-income families, with a new family premium being paid in addition to the basic premium. They will still receive free school meals. There will be a one-parent premium paid on top of this in recognition of the additional problems faced by single parents.

Statutory time off for all pregnant women to attend antenatal clinics was introduced in 1980. Significant improvements in social security provision for women were introduced in 1983. From November in that year a married woman drawing unemployment or sickness benefit was enabled to draw additions for her dependent husband or children. The Conservative Government also extended the right for women with invalidity pensions to receive additional benefits for a dependent husband and children, and a wife became entitled to claim supplementary benefit for the couple as well as a husband. From the same date a working wife gained the right to claim family income supplement on the same terms as her husband. Since 1979 FIS has increased by 10 per cent in real terms.

The old maternity grant of £25, paid to all mothers since 1982, is worth less than £5 at 1969 prices. From April 1987 it will cease to be paid to all mothers and instead a much enhanced maternity grant of £80 will be paid to mothers in receipt of FIS or supplementary benefit. A new statutory maternity pay scheme is also being introduced. Where a woman has been employed by the same employer for at least two years she will get 90% of her average weekly earnings for the first six weeks, and a flat rate of £32.85 for the next twelve weeks. Where a woman has been employed for between six months and two years by the same employer she will get all eighteen weeks at the flat rate of £32.85.

The whole tenor of the new social security provisions is to target help towards low-income families.

A consultative paper on proposals for the establishment of a Family Court was published by the Government in May 1986. Most Conservatives will agree on the need to avoid the often adversarial, fragmented and complicated approach to family matters, including divorce, adoption, wardship and inheritance, which seems inevitable under the present system. Conciliation, and the possibility of rational agreements on the care of children and the division of property, are important objectives in any new proposals. The CWNC has expressed its wholehearted commitment to the concept of family courts.

The Matrimonial and Family Proceedings Act 1984 lays down that when a marriage ends, the interests of the children should be regarded as the first priority. Divorce rates are continuing their inexorable climb: 160,000 in 1980; 175,000 in 1985. Nineteen per cent of all babies born in the UK are now born to unmarried mothers. More than 80 per cent of women under twenty who become pregnant are unmarried. Even if many of these women are in stable relationships, the increasing number of single parents – generally the mother – bringing up children alone is a profound cause for concern.

Although housing is frequently available – to the often expressed irritation of couples waiting on the council list for many years before they can marry or start a family – single-parent families are almost invariably less well off financially, and children growing up without fathers may have a harder time adjusting to the adult world. Boys and young men must be encouraged to share fully the responsibility for their children, and to take seriously the challenges of a mature married relationship.

Under the present Government, one-parent benefit has been at its highest ever level in real terms. Other initiatives include the entitlement to claim the long-term rate of supplementary benefit after one year instead of two as under the previous Government. A single parent also has half his or her earnings between £4 and £20 disregarded and needs to work for only 24 hours, rather than 30, to qualify for FIS. This lower minimum working hours requirement will be the norm for the new family credit.

It is vitally important for government policies not to add to the destabilising of marriage but rather to support it. The family relationships which surround every marriage – whether with children, aunts, cousins or sisters-in-law – remain the most significant and enduring threads in most people's lives. If young people are avoiding marriage to maximise their tax benefits there must be something amiss. There has not been such a great change over the last twenty years, however. In 1985 around three-quarters of the population still lived in families headed by a married couple. The 'familistic social structure' described by Professor Halsey in *Social Trends** is more fragile, with more one-person households, often of elderly people, and many more re-marriages, but it is still the ideal most people strive for.

Health and Safety Compared with 1978, there are now an additional 58,000 nurses and midwives and an additional 3500 GPs. The average number of patients per GP has come down from 2290 in 1976 to 2010 in 1985. The birth rate is relatively stable, except among older women between thirty-five and thirty-nine years of age who are having more children, presumably as a result of the welcome trend to later marriage, and women's wish to establish themselves in their career before starting a family. A girl born today can expect to live until she is at least seventy-seven, compared with a life expectancy of only fifty-two years at the turn of the century. An extra twenty-five years for work and leisure. The four-generation family is back on the agenda.

In October 1986 the Conservative Government appointed a minister with special responsibility for women's health – the first UK Government to take such a step. Apart from child-birth, the health areas of special importance to women include the treatment and prevention of cervical and breast cancer. The number of cervical smear tests increased from 2.8 million in 1976 to 4.3 million in 1985, but the death rate has

* Op. cit., HMSO, 1987.

only shown a slight decline. In 1986 the Secretary of State for Health and Social Security announced a drive for more cervical smears, and in February 1987 asked the health authorities to extend the new computerised call and recall systems for cervical cancer screening to women aged twenty and over. There is increasing concern over the numbers of young women in their twenties with a form of cervical cancer which progresses rapidly and is thought to be associated with early and promiscuous sexual activity. Moral and practical pressures for chastity and fidelity are combining in the eighties to offer at least the possibility of a more responsible and caring society.

In February 1987 Norman Fowler accepted the recommendations of the Government working party on breast cancer and announced the implementation of a national programme for breast cancer screening by X-ray – mammography – for all women aged between fifty and sixty-four, with significant additional funding. The Government is also supporting a ten-year study on thermographic detection of breast cancer. New developments in the detection of ovarian cancer and in the detection of breast cancer by teledianography, offer considerable hope that more resources could now really reduce the tragic mortality rates in these fields.

Kerb crawling was made an offence in the 1985 Sexual Offences Act introduced by Janet Fookes. Local authorities now have the power to limit and license sex shops in their area, and the change in Soho is remarkable.

In 1986 the Government announced that child victims of physical or sexual abuse would be able to give their evidence in court via a live video link. More severe penalties in cases of rape are also strongly supported by Conservatives of both sexes, and the maximum penalty for attempted rape has been increased to life imprisonment. The DHSS helps to fund a number of voluntary rape crisis centres, as well as the Women's Aid Federation which supports refuges for battered women and their children.

Women in general share a profound concern about increasing violence against women, and believe that certain publications and broadcasting material may be encouraging the trend. The Video Recordings Act of 1984 ensured that all videos available for sale or rent must be classified by the British Board of Film Classification and this is having a significant effect on reducing the number of 'video nasties' available.

Many attempts over the years have been made to reform the Obscene Publications Act. Looking towards the 1990s and the vast growth in material that will be beamed into our homes by satellites controlled by other nations, we must persevere in our efforts to find a more easily applied standard for material which is offensive or excessively violent.

Women at Work   In their working role, women are still to a certain extent getting over the effects of the Industrial Revolution.

When mass production was introduced and great factories were built, the workplace became divorced from the domestic or local environment. Before that, spinning, weaving, dyeing and making up would generally take place in the home. As far back as the Middle Ages the nature of these trades was very much a family affair. As Margaret Wade Labarge pointed out in *Women in Medieval Life*,* contemporary sources emphasised the importance of the wife's supervisory and financial role; minding the shop, minding the apprentices – boys and girls – and sharing in the work. When a big order had to be completed the whole family turned to. Many widows continued their husband's businesses in the 13th and 14th centuries, as vintners, brewers, bookbinders or stonemasons, and were admitted to membership of the guilds.

In rural areas, too, the centre of production was the home. Although the rural housewife had clearly defined duties, she also had a generally supervisory role, and at harvest time or in a crisis whole families turned out together to get the work done. Indeed, farmers' wives do the same today and 70 per cent of them do the farm accounts.

---

* Margaret Wade Labarge, *Women in Medieval Life* (Hamish Hamilton, 1986).

Many factors in the 1980s have brought the workplace nearer to the home again, and provided married women with a far wider range of opportunities to combine the earning and the domestic side of their lives. Production units are smaller, the service industries offer flexible working hours and opportunities for part-time work, new technology provides the facility to carry out work from home or any other base, and market towns have re-emerged as pleasant and possible places in which to live and work.

On another front, it is vitally important for overseas development aid programmes not to repeat the negative side of our Industrial Revolution, by letting women's traditional trading and commercial skills be taken over by training schemes and job developments centred on men. Once again, this could lead to the isolation of women in an impoverished domestic environment.

The natural pattern of many modern women's lives – education, first job/training, marriage and children, return to work part-time, perhaps a period of re-training followed by full-time work – chimes increasingly with new patterns in men's lives. Job changes, periods of study or re-training, flexi-hours and independent work from home, including second jobs, have broken up the traditional male pattern of one job for life with a pension attached.

One of the most successful of the Government's employment measures has been the Enterprise Allowance, under which unemployed people who put up their own capital of £1000 are eligible for an allowance of £40 a week and advice and support in the setting up of their business. About 25 per cent of these allowances go to women.

A quarter, or 640,000, of all self-employed people are women, and in the last three years there has been a remarkable 42 per cent increase in the number of women starting up their own firms. Over one quarter of sole proprietorships in the UK are now in the hands of women (up from under 5 per cent in 1972) – a remarkable growth rate but one that still needs nurturing.

In 1985 one third of the places on Manpower Services

Commission (MSC) Business Training Courses were taken up by women. David Trippier, the minister responsible for small firms, is heading a drive to increase the numbers of women entrepreneurs still further. He wants more women as counsellors in the Government-backed Small Firms Service, and as directors of the many new Local Enterprise Agencies. The number of Local Enterprise Agencies, supported by big firms and local professionals, which help and advise small businesses, has gone up from around 23 four years ago, to 328 today.

The Department of Employment is jointly funding a research study on the particular problems women may have in setting up small businesses, and how they manage to stay in business longer, on average, than men. Two new organisations, Women in Enterprise in Wakefield, and the Women's Enterprise Development Agency at Aston, are particularly concerned with the need for women counsellors, such as accountants and bankers, to support women in the construction of their business plans, accounting systems, and in their efforts to get funding for their projects on equal terms with men.

Many of the burdens on small businesses have been removed. Penal taxation on family businesses has been slashed. The national insurance surcharge has been abolished. Multi-rate VAT has gone. A special unit has been set up to scrap or simplify millions of Government forms. The Business Expansion Scheme and the Small Firms Loan Guarantee Scheme have shone the spotlight of success on small businesses, and the men and women – such as Anita Roddick and Jennifer d'Abo – who turn them into big business.

As Leah Hertz points out in her book *The Business Amazons*,* women can be particularly successful given the autonomy to run their own show. A majority of the women she spoke to started their businesses after getting married or

---

* Leah Hertz, *The Business Amazons* (André Deutsch, 1986).

having children. As a teacher before our first child was born, and a self-starting, self-stopping part-timer afterwards, I know the delights of taking a day off to make marmalade and catching up on the paperwork next week.

The move away from an increasingly collectivist state, where escalating numbers of the population were employed by Government or public agencies with terms and conditions of work set centrally, to the new entrepreneurial culture, where patterns of work to suit individuals or local circumstances can take over, is nothing but good news for women who want to earn their living but retain some control over the quality of their lives. The impact on children of seeing the world of work at first hand, with both parents involved, can be a positive introduction to the grown-up world.

Two of the most significant trends for women in employment have come in the phenomenal growth of women entering the professions, and in the development of the tourism and leisure sector.

Within the professions, girls have clearly identified the high earnings and the freedom of operation which a professional person can command. Forty-nine per cent of those accepted to read law at universities in 1986 were women, and 40 per cent of entrants to the legal profession are women. There are about 1400 women partners in solicitors' firms, almost 7 per cent of the total, and the number is increasing each year. They leave to have children but increasingly return to work after a short break, often initially to shorter hours. Forty-six per cent of those accepted to read medicine at university in 1986 were women. Over 20 per cent of GPs in England in 1984 were women, though they only made up about 11 per cent of hospital consultants. In 1985 32 per cent of the students starting chartered accountancy training were women. Some 25 per cent of those obtaining their banking diplomas in 1986 were women, but the number of women running bank branches is still infinitesimal.

There are still significant invisible barriers to women getting ahead in long-established traditional fields of employment. Anything slightly resembling a closed shop, whether it's a trade union or a profession, will seek to protect the interests of its current membership. Only by getting in there in large numbers, as they are doing, and becoming a significant force, will young women ever get the chance to come up on the inside track like the favoured young men in the past.

One of the factors prevalent in the new business culture that works effectively for women's advancement, particularly in the new financial services sector, is payment by results. Sales executives can be judged precisely by their sales, and one of the all-time top earners in the insurance industry in recent years was a young woman.

In the development of leisure and tourism, Government policy has featured strongly: minimum interference, support for international marketing, development funds of £35 million over the last four years, and the establishment of new training courses, including 11,000 Youth Training Scheme (YTS) places, to improve standards at all levels. Leisure and tourism, including the hotel and catering industry, offer significant growth in jobs for people ranging from the unskilled to the graduate trainee. Many of them are particularly easy for women to enter. In the growing market for conferences and group visits, many companies were started by women in a back room at home, and have since developed into highly successful and internationally reputable businesses. Prue Leith of the Leith Catering Group, Laura Morgan, past Chairman of the British Incoming Tour Operators' Association and Managing Director of International Vacationers, Anthea Fortescue of Conference Associates, Joan Wilkins of Conferences and Communications, Michelle Berriedale-Johnson of Catercall and Annabel Geddes, who established the London Dungeon, are just a few examples. Half the managers at the London Tourist Board when I chaired it were women. Tourism is one of the more gender blind industries I've come across.

Before the last war, a woman was expected to resign her job in a public service such as the Foreign Office, in a bank or other major company, when she got married. This is certainly no longer the case, but marriage will always continue to have more impact on the lives of women than on those of men. As the Government's *Social Trends* survey* shows, washing and ironing are shared equally by only 9 per cent of married couples, cooking by 16 per cent, cleaning by 23 per cent and shopping by 39 per cent. Surprisingly it is older men in their forties who contribute most to domestic tasks, or perhaps they have less hang-ups about admitting it.

Partnership doesn't have to mean each partner doing half of everything, but it does mean a freely agreed share-out of all the tasks to be done, and a preparedness to renegotiate that share-out at regular intervals.

It's here that a closer examination of the breakdown of the figures on women at work is particularly interesting. If you look at the 1985 statistics for the sixteen million women of working age (sixteen to fifty-nine) you see that over five million – 33.6 per cent – do no paid work, 31 per cent work full-time, 23.7 per cent part-time, 3.9 per cent are self-employed, and 6.8 per cent are seeking work. A higher percentage of British women work than in any other country in the EEC except for Denmark.

So 66.4 per cent of women of working age are at work or seeking work, but less than one third of women in the UK work full-time.

For married women the importance of part-time work is extremely significant. In 1984 only 25 per cent of married women aged between sixteen and fifty-nine worked full-time, and more, 31 per cent, worked part-time. Of the 7.2 million mothers with dependent children in 1985, a mere 16.2 per cent worked full-time, 33.2 per cent part-time and over three million mothers (43.7 per cent) did not work or seek work.

So in every one of the following groups of women of working age, even mothers with dependent children, the majority are at work, but among married women the number of part-timers still clearly exceeds the full-timers. Hence the central significance for married women of the growing number of part-time jobs.

---

* Op. cit., HMSO, 1987.

	Work full-time	Work part-time	Economically active, incl. self-employed and those seeking work	Not economically active	Source
All women, 16–59 [15.874 million]	31%	23.7%	66.4%	33.6%	*Social Trends '87* + Labour Force Survey '85
Single women, 16–59	53%	5%	71%	29%	General Household Survey '84
All married women, 16–59	25%	31%	61%	39%	General Household Survey '84
Mothers with dependent children [7.249 million]	16.2%	33.2%	56.3%	43.7%	Labour Force Survey '85

After raising a family many women may need to rebuild their confidence and learn new skills in a rapidly changing job scene. In 1986 3000 women were helped by the Wider Opportunities for Women (WOW) courses run by the MSC. The MSC has also funded the Women in Technology scheme run by the Open University.

I have already emphasised the importance of Career-Break programmes offering reinstatement for mothers, such as those run by the banks and the civil service. The figures above highlight the importance of part-time work in women's lives, and the need to ensure that it remains widely available in large and small businesses. Some companies have already moved to provide part-timers with pro-rata pension rights and other benefits.

In 1982 the Government announced a grant to employers who set up appropriate Job Splitting schemes. This served to focus employers' attention on the potential advantages for them and their staff, and many more employers are now operating job-share schemes, predominantly for women. Job-sharing provides prospects, pay and benefits in line with full-time work.

The Government has extended the scope of the Sex Discrimination Act to cover firms employing five or less staff and repealed outdated restrictions on women's hours and conditions of work. Women's hourly earnings have crept up to 74·1 per cent of men's* and the 1984 Equal Pay Amendment Act now allows claims for equal pay for work of equal value.

Discussions on the most equitable way to harmonise the retirement ages of men and women in the state pensions scheme continue. However, the vast cost of full equality for men and women at sixty (estimated at £3bn), and the inevitable detriment to women currently at work of suggesting that they should have a reduced pension between the ages of sixty and sixty-five, are formidable barriers.

The Equal Opportunities Commission, under the chairmanship of Baroness Platt, continues to do a good and necessary job of work. Fully supported by the Government, it has substantial powers to lean on employers and others when traditionalists forget or choose to ignore the new rules on just treatment, embodied in their Code of Practice, approved by Parliament in 1985.

I believe, with the Government, and most Conservatives, that in the interests of justice and the nation's need, all doors in the world of work should be open to women on equal terms with men. I also believe that in response to women's own wishes, and the needs of their families and children, it must be possible for women to spend as much time as they choose as 'Household Managers', returning to work when or if their responsibilities permit; and that tax, training and social security systems should support and facilitate, not hinder, this vital flexibility.

Tax The report 'Women and Tax' was produced in 1979 by the CWNC. It stressed the need to make women independent entities for tax purposes, whether married or single, with or without earned income. It considered that each spouse should

---

Employment Gazette, 1987.

be responsible for declaring their own income and paying their own tax.

The 1979 report, and a CWNC working party's response in 1981 to the Government Green Paper 'The Taxation of Husband and Wife', expressed the belief that the tax system should not try either to discourage or encourage married women to take paid work. They came out against the anomaly of the married man's tax allowance, and in favour of a system of mandatory independent taxation, where both partners in all marriages would receive the single person's tax allowance, which could be transferable between husband and wife if one partner earned less than the allowance.

It was considered that this would be the fair middle course between the present alternatives of two and a half times the single allowance for two-wage couples (i.e. the married man's tax allowance plus the wife's earned income allowance), and one and a half times the single person's allowance (i.e. the married man's tax allowance) where only the husband earns. There is actually an odd quirk in the system which gives two and a half times the single tax allowance to married couples where only the wife is earning. A revised tax system should be totally non-discriminatory with regard to men and women.

Conservative women believe it is important for the tax system to continue to take into account the many couples where only one partner is earning, and the husband or wife chooses to stay at home – taking a career break to help with children or dependent relatives, or to study – and to recognise the contribution to the family, and the permanent earnings loss suffered by the women, or men, who do so. Figures published by the Equal Opportunities Commission show that 39 per cent of married women of working age are not economically active, while an additional 31 per cent work part-time. The present system and Opposition proposals actually penalise the family whose income declines when a wife stops work just when they need most help.

Under a system of transferable allowance, all married women earning over the tax threshold (£2425 in 1987/8) would have full privacy in their tax affairs. Only for husbands or wives with less income than this each year, or with no income, would optional transferability involve them in informing their partner of the level of their income, if they wanted the benefits of transferability.

In an analysis by the EOC in 1982, support for a system of fully or partially transferable allowances came not only from the CWNC, but from twelve other bodies, including the Institute of Taxation, the Law Society, the UK Federation of Business and Professional Women and the Women's National Commission.

It is misleading to argue that transferability would discourage married women from returning to work. You could equally argue that the present system of aggregation holds down women's wages, discouraging them from earning over £2425.

The incomes of a married couple are normally aggregated for tax purposes. The wife's earnings, after deduction of her tax allowance, will effectively be taxed at her husband's top rate. Even if they join the small minority of couples who elect to surrender the married man's allowance and be taxed as two single people on their earnings, the wife's investment income will still be added to her husband's income, and taxed at his top rate.

The CWNC believes that each spouse should be taxed separately on their investment income as well as their earned income. Considerable resentment is felt by very many women who have built up their own savings and find that on marriage they are penalised.

Following the Green Paper on Personal Taxation published by the Chancellor in March 1986, the CWNC launched a major national survey. Questionnaires from 3254 people, men as well as women, were returned from a wide range of sources, including the *Sunday Times* and *Cosmopolitan* magazine, which had reprinted the form. There was a high level of awareness and understanding of the proposals. An overwhelming majority thought the married man's tax allowance and the aggregation of the wife's investment income with her husband's unfair. Seventy per cent favoured transferable allowances.

The CWNC strongly supports the present Government's drive to reduce direct taxation and looks forward to progress in the introduction of a system of equal tax treatment for both partners in a marriage. The debate continues, centring on the importance of even-handed treatment of men and women, privacy, and the administrative costs of any new system. Few commentators speak up for the many women at home.

Only one capital gains tax allowance and only one set of tax relief on mortgage interest is allowed to a married couple, while two single people can get one each. On top of this, the fact that a married woman's savings income is taxed at her husband's top rate is currently encouraging a lot of high-earning young people (the DINKies or Dual Income No Kids) to opt out of marriage. I doubt if our tax system intended this to happen.

Women in the Community   Here I shall bring together other aspects of women at home such as care of elderly or handicapped relatives, those who are themselves disabled, the retired, and the vitally important voluntary sector.

Fifty-one per cent of adult women of all ages are not economically active – that's about eleven million adult women in the community, many of course looking after young children. The role of caring for disabled or elderly relatives also still generally falls to women. Spending on cash benefits for long-term sick and disabled people has improved by 55 per cent in real terms since 1978/79. The mobility allowance was made tax free from April 1982 as recommended by the CWNC Budget submission, in particular helping disabled people who go out to work. The invalid care allowance (ICA), paid to men and single women under pension age who look after a severely disabled person, was introduced in 1976 by the Labour Government. Its scope was extended in 1981 by the Conservative Government to non-relatives, and since 1979 its basic rate has more than doubled. The CWNC lobbied for a number of years to extend the ICA to married women and this has now been done under the 1986 Social Security Act and backdated to December 1984.

In 1984 a major new benefit, the severe disablement

allowance (SDA), replaced the non-contributory invalidity pension and the separate housewives' non-contributory invalidity pension, which discriminated against married women. SDA is paid on equal terms to both sexes. An additional 20,000 people were expected to benefit from the introduction of SDA, at an initial cost of £20 million.

There are many more women pensioners than men. By November 1986, pensions had risen by 98 per cent since 1978/79 – more than the rate of inflation. Since 1979, pensioners have been granted a special Christmas bonus every year (the Labour Government did not pay it in 1975 and 1976), and pensioners can now earn up to £75 per week without any deduction of pension. Small pensioner households also benefit from rating reform proposals.

Under the new 1986 Social Security Act, the state will continue to provide basic pensions fully protected against price rises, but for the first time everyone will have the freedom to choose the kind of pension they want on top of that provided by the state.

The Conservative Government has ensured that increases in war widows' pensions are exempted from income tax, so remedying a long-standing grievance whereby, although the husband's war disability pension was not subject to tax, his widow's pension was. Increases in war widows' pensions have kept well ahead of inflation, and the same is true of the widow's pension payable under the national insurance scheme.

The new Social Security Act will concentrate help on widows who are most in need, and at the time they need it most. They will receive a £1000 lump sum immediately after bereavement to replace the widow's allowance at present paid for the first six months of widowhood. Widowed mother's allowance, and widow's pension will be paid immediately on bereavement instead of after six months. The age at which widow's pension is paid will be increased by five years in order to concentrate help on older widows who are less likely to be working.

The case for voluntary organisations was made by the late Lord Beveridge when he wrote: 'In a totalitarian society all action outside the citizen's home . . . is directed or controlled by the State. By contrast, vigour and abundance of Voluntary Action, individually and in association with other citizens, for bettering one's own life and that of one's fellows, are the distinguishing marks of a free society.'*

The voluntary sector has been encouraged to expand considerably under the present Government. Since 1979 the central government grant to the voluntary sector has more than doubled, reaching £224 million in 1984–5. In 1983 the timespan for covenanting to charitable organisations was reduced from seven years to four.

An additional and powerful incentive to voluntary effort came with the 1986 Budget. This introduced the radical new system of payroll giving to allow people at work to contribute a regular sum to charity from their pre-tax earnings. The same budget gave public companies the right to make single gifts to charities tax free, up to an amount equal to 3 per cent of dividends payable to shareholders.

The Government's new Helping the Community to Care initiative was launched in July 1984, with a commitment of £10.5 million over three years, to help volunteers, families and others to care for people who need support. It is currently aiding a project for self-help family centres which will have £500,000 in funds over three years. This is in line with a major element in Conservative thinking which is to encourage care for the individual at home or in the local community, rather than in large impersonal institutions.

Women are active in all sorts of voluntary movements, as carers, campaigners and activists, from the famous Women's Royal Voluntary Service (WRVS) to CRUSE (the organisation to help the widowed), NAWCH, the National Association for the Welfare of Children in Hospital, PPA, the Pre-School Playgroups Association and the National Trust, as well as the many activities centred on the Church. Out and about during the day, being good neighbours, women are often the binding

---

*Lord Beveridge, *Voluntary Action* (Allen & Unwin, 1948).

force that holds a community together. Although men and young people are increasingly active in the volunteer movement, and businesses are giving more assistance in cash and in kind, it still largely depends upon women. We must be wary of asking too much of them without providing the necessary support.

Women of Influence Seeing women regularly take up powerful or influential positions – or seeing men in humane and caring roles – is good for all of us, men and women, boys and girls. Open doors extend our range of options and take the blinkers off our eyes. Every time we see a doctor who is a woman, a professor, an MP or councillor, a camera operator, or a judge, all women, and all there on merit, it helps erode the still too prevalent conception that such jobs are really for men. The tiny number of women at the top – still only 2 per cent of directorships are held by women – is increasingly coming under pressure from the rapidly growing numbers of women in professional or management jobs – currently around 25 per cent.

Ensuring that women are treated fairly on the path to the top cannot just be left to the law and the Equal Opportunities Commission. All of us need to look carefully at the images of women we put out on the television screen, in advertisements, in material for young people, in recruitment notices. I also believe that the way we use language does matter and, however subtly, can put across the message to girls that it's still a man's world, and that women come after. 'The male embraces the female,' as the lawyers still say.

I confess I can't get worked up about the use of 'Chairman' or 'mankind', but I do wince a bit at being addressed as 'gentlemen', 'Dear Sir', or being told that there is only one woman in a four-man crew. Does that make it a crew of five? After all, even Jenny Wren in Dickens' *Our Mutual Friend* declares 'I am the person of the house.'

When standing orders state that 'a member shall take his seat . . .' it is quite possible to follow Dr Radcliffe Richards' suggestion to extend the use of the neutral 'they' ('their') as a singular pronoun. Even Jane Austen did this, and I have taken advantage of the usage several times in this essay. Of course we already use the plural 'you' as a singular pronoun to replace 'thou'.

Image and expectations have a profound effect on behaviour.

One area in which government can act positively to open doors and use the skills of women is in appointments to public bodies. Only about one in seven public appointments go to women. The Prime Minister has made it plain that she has asked all government ministers to include women's names on shortlists for public appointments submitted to her, and has also asked the civil service to re-examine the current make-up of publicly appointed bodies.

To say that women do not help women is certainly not my experience. My first three major appointments all came directly through women friends and colleagues. The great range of networking groups set up by women for women, from the Women's Institute, through the Soroptimists, to Women in Media and the new Network, all give important opportunities for women to establish friendships and broaden their horizons.

Some of the most impressive gains for women have been in the field of local government. Over 38 per cent of all Surrey county councillors are women, and five out of their eleven main committees are chaired by women. In England and Wales 25 per cent of Conservative councillors are women, an increase from 18 per cent in 1977.

Many women fulfil an important and influential role as magistrates. Over 40 per cent of magistrates on the active list are now women. Many of these women who are councillors, magistrates, or who serve on public bodies, are part of that significant group of 'household managers' who often earn nothing for their work.

We still have to learn to value experience in the home and the community more highly, and to extend power to people who represent the many who do not at the moment, for whatever reason, work full-time.

In the House of Lords there are many women from a broad

range of experience who have been appointed life peers under the Conservative Government, to enable them to play an influential part in national affairs.

In the House of Commons there are now 28 women MPs out of 650: a tiny 4 per cent of the total, and still below the record 29 returned in 1964. Fourteen of them are Conservatives, of whom four are ministers and two parliamentary private secretaries. We now have two husband and wife teams in Parliament, both Conservative, and in 1983 Conservatives Sally and Phillip Oppenheim became the first mother and son to sit together in the House of Commons, just as Diana Elles and her son James are a first in the European Parliament.

In 1919 the first woman to take her seat in Parliament was the Conservative Lady Astor. The first woman to occupy the Speaker's Chair was Conservative MP Bettie Harvie Anderson and Janet Young was the first woman Leader of the House of Lords. In February 1975 the Right Honourable Margaret Thatcher was elected leader of the Conservative Party – the first woman politician of any party in the western democratic world to be so elected. Following the General Election in May 1979 she became Britain's first woman Prime Minister.

The impact of Mrs Thatcher's election as party leader and her position as Prime Minister has been immense. The visual message of seeing a woman leading the nation continuously for eight years tells girls and young women more effectively than any statements of intent that the doors are open to the very top.

When I saw the Head of a Middle Eastern State welcomed at Victoria Station some years ago by our Head of State Her Majesty Queen Elizabeth, our Prime Minister the Right Honourable Margaret Thatcher, and the Lord Lieutenant of London Baroness Phillips, I can't have been the only one to feel a certain amount of pride.

Conclusion

Within the family structure, a topic which tends to come up when policies which matter to women are discussed, home is central. Not just the abstract concept of 'a home', but the roof over our heads and the four walls that give us privacy and security. Learning care and respect for others and for their property comes with learning care and respect for ourselves and our own property, and that starts in our own home.

The security of owning your own home – a central part of Conservative policy over the years – gives point and purpose to everything that happens in it. The right to buy, and low-cost home ownership schemes means that we have one of the highest percentages of home ownership in Europe – 64 per cent. Housing probably impacts more on women than on men. Whether a woman spends her day working there, or locks the front door on it on her way out to work, a good and secure home environment certainly makes her life easier.

But progress is not just about making life easier. Perhaps I've looked too much on the bright side. But when you consider the vast improvements in women's opportunities which have arisen since we all got the vote in 1928, the speed of change has been phenomenal. This has been helped to a certain extent by specific policies directed to women, but more often than not by the march of science, and by women themselves, together with men of foresight, who have pressed for change and improvement, for the sake of their daughters if not themselves.

A study in America showed that when the chairman or chief executive's daughters finally came through their long and expensive education and moved into the job market, opportunities for women in his company suddenly multiplied. We can still multiply the opportunities for women – in wage levels, in seniority, in options for parents to care for their own children. But options are seldom easy to decide between. The more choices we have, the harder the decision. Conservative policy aims to see that the doors are open, and to let people choose for themselves.

Recognising the Dual Role of Women

Jane Ewart-Biggs

'Women make up half of the world's population, perform two-thirds of the world's work and receive one tenth of its income.' These facts, from a United Nations source, can only mean there are still women all over the world who are exploited, disadvantaged and discriminated against. The purpose of this essay is to examine the situation of women in Britain today and some of the ways in which a Labour Government would act to make their lives fairer and happier. I shall consider the barriers that women face in their pursuit of equality and justice, but at the same time look at the wider framework in which both men and women function. For in order to widen the choices open to women, we must first decide how best to adjust the laws and institutions which embrace men and women and how best to influence those firmly entrenched attitudes regarding the roles that men and women have traditionally occupied.

I am writing this essay from the viewpoint of a socialist and I shall, at the outset, touch on the philosophy which underlies socialist theories on how to structure society for the benefit of all. Our aim is to see a society where each individual is enabled to contribute to the best of his or her ability and where the available goods and services are distributed to satisfy the basic needs of everyone. For people to achieve their potential it is not only necessary for them to acquire food, warmth and shelter, but also to benefit from the pride and dignity that flows from a positive image of themselves and others. Self-image is a powerful force and starts to form early in life. How our parents treated us as babies, our pre-school experience, our formal and informal education, how our colleagues see us, the effect the neighbourhood we live in has on us – all these, and many other factors, exercise a lasting influence on our expectations and the image we have of ourselves.

These self-images are also affected by how society, through its policies, its laws, its ways of operating and its media, project us. I shall try to illustrate how – for most women – society imposes a different image and set of expectations for women than for their male counterparts.

There are many groups of women, and any one woman may define herself in a number of different ways. For example, she may see herself as a shop assistant, a trade unionist, a daughter, a wife, a mother, a school governor, a Samaritan, an 'O' level student, and so on, all at the same time. In many of these roles she will be part of groups made up of both men and women and in some her role and that of her male counterpart will barely differ. Yet, for most women, both their total 'package' of roles and the specifics of each of them will tend to have characteristics regarded as distinctive to women.

People are not able to give of their best when basic needs remain unmet and they cannot make their most valuable contribution when feeling undervalued themselves. The last eight years – the most recent span of Tory rule in Britain – has seen the poor become poorer, social and welfare services curtailed and unemployment soar. In this essay I wish to show how women, occupying a vulnerable position within society, have borne much of the brunt of this deterioration. I will then point to some key policies which an incoming Labour Government would introduce to redress the balance.

Employment and Education

But, first, what are the major factors which determine a woman's place in society, and where does society itself perceive that place to be? A woman's distinctive biological function is to bear and suckle children. Thereafter, the responsibility of being the major caring parent is invested in her. Always, from a small girl onwards, she is taught to feel that her first obligation is to her child and even to more tenuously connected relatives. She must regard other activities, including paid employment, as secondary to the domestic or caring role. Men, on the other hand, are conditioned into precisely the reverse set of priorities; willingness to take on 'caring' roles is seen as a hallmark of 'womanliness'.

By saying this I do not mean that I take exception to the encouragement of women holding caring attitudes towards the vulnerable; of course not. But what I can and do take exception to is the difference in expectation of such attitudes as between men and women, and to the fact that the freedom of one sex is extended by limiting that of the other. Nor can I accept the exploitation of women's caring as an alternative to the provision of proper levels of health and welfare services. Perhaps, most fundamentally of all, it is totally unacceptable that a workplace structure should give diminished rights and status to those who have caring obligations.

Looking back over this century, we cannot fail to recognise how, whereas a man's position with his right to paid employment has been regarded as inflexible, a woman's role has been adjusted according to what society requires of her. The ease with which British governments have found themselves capable of adjusting to differing and conflicting theories of childcare in the light of differing demands on women's labour is especially noteworthy.

In Victorian times, society's view was that she was needed in the home, was expected to bear large numbers of children and to run the house. Queen Victoria herself said: 'Let a woman be what God intended, a helpmate for man, but with totally different duties and vocations.' Those duties and vocations were principally childcare and running a home.

During the two World Wars, women were brought back into the labour force in the need to swell numbers in the munition factories to help with the war effort. Not only did it suddenly become possible to provide nurseries, but it also became the acceptable theory that young children benefited from long periods spent apart from their mothers.

The position has once again been reversed. The recession

has propelled many women back into the home, with many others made to feel that they should relinquish their demands on the shrinking labour market for the benefit of male 'heads of families'. And, as a final encouragement, moral arguments are put forward by Government and the Conservative press that the cohesion of the family depends on the woman's presence at home. Once again, a mother's absence from the home is held responsible for a multitude of sins from family breakdown to juvenile crime.

The reality is that the division of the woman's role between home and place of paid employment remains conveniently ambiguous, so that she may be pushed and pulled in whatever direction is felt necessary by economic policy makers. I believe little or nothing has been done by the present Government to improve the position and, when in years to come we look back at the present time, it may well seem a strange paradox that the first ever government to be led by a woman has seen a continued narrowing of the options open to working women and a further undermining of her stability in the workplace. For at no point does the present Government's record display enough sympathy and support for the Prime Minister's peers and contemporaries who, like herself, also happen to be working family women.

The extent of the movement of women – particularly married women – in and out of work is a factor which should influence the policies affecting their lives, so I will briefly review the fluctuation of that movement during this century.

It is estimated that in 1921 married women formed 3.8 per cent of the workforce, rising to 11.8 per cent in 1951, and 25.9 per cent in 1981. This steady rise has been maintained and now, women as a whole – working either full-time or part-time – form approximately 43 per cent of the total labour force, with as much as 66 per cent of all married women having jobs, although most of them are part-time. This has brought about a change to the prototype family structure of a working husband, economically inactive wife and two dependent children. And, although so much of our fiscal and social security legislation has evolved to match that family structure, only around 5 per cent of the households in the country conform to it at the present time.

A recent 'Women and Employment' study found that, overall, women are spending an increasing proportion of their lives in employment, although very few adopt the typical male pattern of continuous lifetime participation in the labour market. Most interruptions to women's working lives are for domestic reasons; it is normal practice for women to work full-time until the birth of their first child. Very high proportions of women return to work after having a child, but this is not a new phenomenon; over 90 per cent of women who first gave birth in the early 1960s returned to work at some stage. What is new is that women are now returning to work more quickly and are increasingly returning to work between births. Also, as their families grow older and more independent, they are likely to have as much as twenty years of full-time work ahead of them.

It is important to correct the myth that women earners are doing jobs for pin money. The reality is that paid employment in the vast majority of cases is a matter of economic necessity. It is estimated that without women's wages, the number of families living below the poverty line would quadruple. And with the divorce rate rising this is a situation which can only worsen.

Although women now form a large part of the labour force it is important to recognise how largely they are concentrated in a narrow range of low-paid and unskilled work. According to last year's Department of Employment survey, about two-thirds of women worked only with women. This indicates that what they were doing could only be described as 'women's work' – namely work which men either cannot or do not want to do: the type of jobs which can be fitted around school hours, caring activities, and so on. With this in mind it is hardly surprising to learn that in 1984, for all full-time female employees, mean earnings were under 66 per cent of those for men.* Thus the type of jobs occupied by women provided them with only two-thirds of the money earned by men working similar hours.

* *Social Trends* No. 16 (HMSO, 1986).

What, then, are the types of jobs taken by women? The fact that women absent themslves from work for the birth of a child brings with it substantial downward occupational mobility, meaning that they are more likely to seek part-time work when they return. Here, structural changes in the economy have brought a growth in such work. While jobs in manufacturing have declined, jobs in the service sector – undoubtedly a sector which favours women – have increased. But even then they are concentrated in only a small number of the occupational categories. This is borne out by the 1981 Office of Population census which showed that two-thirds of women in paid work belong to only three of the eighteen occupational groupings. These are clerical jobs (33 per cent), service sector jobs (23 per cent) and professional jobs (14 per cent), generally in positions with a low status. For example, service sector jobs include charwomen, office cleaners and canteen assistants and, even in the professional category, the positions taken by women are more likely to be the minor ones, like librarianship and teaching. Moreover, although half of Britain's teachers are women, their positions relate to the lower levels of the hierarchy. Over three-quarters of them work in primary schools and, although women provide as much as 46 per cent of teachers in secondary schools, it was reported by the National Union of Teachers in the early 1980s that they provided only 1 per cent of head teachers.

We are therefore forced to conclude that with the concentration of women in a few categories of occupation – and generally at a lower level – a sexual division of labour exists. The type of jobs only done by women tends to mirror the unpaid work they do at home. Thus, their occupation both in the workplace and at home revolves round looking after children, looking after men, preparing and serving meals and generally clearing up after people. Studies of women's work have even suggested that office work is the business equivalent of housework, that filing documents is as repetitious and tedious as washing dishes. Seen in this way, the sexual division of labour at work is simply an extension of the division of labour at home, leading to the conclusion that

women have acquired a 'dual role' in which they combine
paid work and the unpaid domestic work of the family. This
modification, rather than a transformation of the sexual
division of labour between men and women, is the crux of
the matter.

The Labour Party believes that changes and improvements
are necessary not only to relieve and support women in their
dual role but also to free them from discrimination and to help
them achieve their full potential both at home and in the
workplace. We believe that the reason they are under pressure
is that more and more are subject to a competitive work ethic
without being relieved of their traditional domestic responsibilities.

Many women, by reason of low pay and inadequate benefits,
are among the poorest in our society. In the last eight years
their situation has worsened as the gap between the rich and
the poor has grown wider. *Social Trends** shows that the
share of income at the bottom 40 per cent of households has
fallen from 10.2 per cent in 1976 to 7 per cent, while the
income share of the top fifth has grown from 44.4 per cent to
48 per cent. An incoming Labour Government will narrow
that gap through its policies on unemployment, pay and the
tax and benefit systems. Its intention to reduce unemployment by one million during its first two years in office will
bring about openings for the 965,400 women whom the
Labour Market Statistics showed as officially unemployed in
December 1986 – although the true figures are probably twice
as high.

But, in addition, measures to ensure that job openings for
women are both realisable and justly rewarded, will have to
be taken: measures involving changes in women's education
and training; increases in childcare facilities; jobs with
shorter and more flexible hours; the introduction of a system
of parental leave, and so on.

In education, girls and women, as pupils and students, have

---

* *Social Trends* No. 16 (HMSO, 1986).

been disproportionately affected by the cuts which have impoverished the education service. With severe pressure on resources and falling rolls, the ability of the school system to overcome sex stereotyping and provide equal opportunities for girls has been severely reduced. Increasing class sizes due to staff shortages have meant that teachers find it harder to direct sufficient attention to the girls – who by their very nature are less demanding than boys – in order to develop their capacity to the full. Fewer girls are being offered subjects such as physics, technology and design, making them more and more the preserve of boys. And a reduction in in-service training means that fewer teachers will be educated to understand the ways in which overt and hidden discrimination affecting girls' performance may be overcome.

When it comes to further education, girls tend to face strong social pressures to finish their education early, marry and have children. As a further disincentive, instead of providing students with adequate maintenance support (student grants have declined in value by 20 per cent since 1979), the Government is planning the introduction of student loans. This would affect girls leaving school even more than boys, as the problems in repaying the loans will be greater for women, who are more likely to be low-paid, to leave work to care for children or to be unemployed than men.

In higher education, the way the cuts are being shared out make it harder for those women wanting to go to university or college. The reason for this is that the University Grants Committee has been protecting science-based courses at the expense of the arts, humanities and social sciences, while more than 60 per cent of women in higher education study arts subjects.

In addition, school-leavers wishing to equip themselves for entry into scientific, technological and engineering courses, but equipped with the wrong 'A' levels, are being denied the opportunity to do so because the conversion courses enabling them to change direction are the very courses which are being cut.

The training opportunities available for women at the

present time are limited. And since women are often less qualified than men and their skills concentrated in a narrow range of jobs, they need training – and retraining – to help them compete for male-dominated jobs and to meet the new technology to which women's jobs are particularly exposed. Even though Britain lags behind its main competitors in training provision, the Government, through its economic strategy, has cut the funds available in industry for training and has launched a direct attack on the training system.

Apprenticeships and other training opportunities for young women are minimal, mainly because they are not encouraged to enter manufacturing industries and often enter service industries which provide very little off-the-job training. In 1981, while there were 210,500 people in manufacturing industry, only 25,000 (12 per cent) of these were female. Meanwhile, cutbacks in teacher training affect women disproportionately since women make up 80 per cent of all students on teacher training courses.

Lastly, the Government's onslaught on the Industrial Training Board system, with sixteen out of twenty-three training boards abolished, will mean a curtailment of the opportunities which these boards offered women.

A Labour Government would remove the inequalities in the education system and improve training opportunities. Funds would be restored to local education authorities in order to reduce class sizes and improve learning materials in primary schools. There would be encouragement towards the attainment of a higher standard of achievement among all pupils in the variety of academic and other activities which are an essential part of fully comprehensive education, and proper financial support for those in post-sixteen education would be guaranteed.

Women would be primarily helped by the restoration of education as a high priority both in terms of profile and funding, but they would benefit further from the changes planned by Labour to make education throughout life a reality. First, the higher education system would be made fairer, with equal funding for the institutions doing equal work. Higher and continuing education would be planned as a whole through a national council.

Second, grants for students would be improved and extended, with educational maintenance allowances paid to those wishing to stay on in full-time education at sixteen.

Third, those adults denied education after the age of eighteen should be offered the chance of an educational entitlement. This would cover one year's education and be backed by financial support.

Lastly, institutions would be encouraged to open their doors to more women from ethnic minority backgrounds. They would offer 'second chance' opportunities for older people through part-time courses, for example. Women whose education would have been more likely to have suffered from discrimination or interruption would in particular benefit from opportunities offered them later in life.

Social and Legal Provisions

I have described how the Labour Party believes that women's employment opportunities can best be furthered by providing improved schooling, further education and training facilities but, at the same time, supportive measures to help women filling the dual role of mother and worker are seen as crucial. Of particular importance are better childcare facilities. In this connection the Labour Party has committed itself to place a statutory duty on local authorities to provide nursery education for all three- or four-year-old children whose parents require it. Moreover, the present Government's refusal to exempt workplace nurseries from tax would be reversed.

Labour also believes in giving legislative support to parents to take a dual responsibility in the upbringing of their children. At present, the UK Government is the only EEC government blocking the parental leave directive. This would give working parents who have a baby the right to take at least three months paid leave during the first two years of the baby's life to look after their child. The directive would not only remove the obvious disadvantage which a female candidate suffers in the eyes of prospective employers but it would also encourage fathers to take a greater part in the upbringing of their children.

A further burden carried by women is the responsibility society vests in them to care for elderly and disabled relatives. The 1980 census of Women and Employment found that nearly one in eight of all women provided essential care for a sick or elderly dependant – over three million women – and that one out of five of these carers felt that their work opportunities had been affected as a result. But although these women carry such a heavy burden, often at grave financial and personal cost to themselves, they receive little support. Three-quarters of them are not visited by a home help, for instance. Two out of three cannot take holidays or go out in the evenings because their dependant needs full-time attention. Indeed it was only when forced by the European Court of Justice that the Tories extended the invalid care allowance to cover married women in addition to men and single women.

A Labour Government would provide support and help to these home carers. Home helps would be made available if needed by the families, as would services such as night sitting and specialist nursing. The means of providing a social life for the elderly and disabled would be available, as well as self-help centres and counselling for carers and their families, and a place to turn in times of crisis.

The Labour Party believes that the only way of shielding women from exploitation and low pay in the workplace is through the introduction of a national minimum wage with statutory backing. Although the level of this minimum is not yet decided – it would be decided following consultation with both union and employers – the suggested amount is £80 per week.

Labour will also act to improve women's rights at work, especially those of part-time workers and home workers, giving them greater job security and better conditions of employment. Policies for the reform of the tax system will also benefit women. Reducing the burden of taxation on the low-paid will increase women's net earnings, and restructuring the system of national insurance contributions will ensure that women in low-paid and part-time jobs are no longer disadvantaged. Plans for independent taxation will treat married couples as equals, giving women greater financial freedom and privacy, and put an end to the assumption that women are their husband's dependants. Improvements in the basic state pension will raise the incomes of many women who, because of a lifetime of low earnings, make up the majority receiving the basic pension level. Labour will retain and improve the state earnings related pension (SERPS), which for many women provides a good, or even the only, opportunity for an addition to the basic pension. And, finally, Labour believes in the need to ensure that women have a genuine right to claim equal pay for work of equal value and that the legislation against sex discrimination in work and training must be strengthened.

Such changes should contribute a great deal towards safeguarding women against poverty. In addition, following the weakening of the machinery to ensure fair wages, steps will be taken to re-establish Fair Wages Resolution provisions and to reinstate those under 21 within the scope of the Wages Council.

There are always lessons to be learned from abroad. In this instance the American policy of contract compliance is judged to have achieved significant success for ethnic minorities and women in the USA. This is a system whereby the US Government uses its purchasing power to attack discrimination in the private sector. Contractors to the US Government are expected to meet certain employment standards and their performance is monitored to ensure that they do so.

In Britain, although successive governments have repeatedly condemned discrimination and brought in initiatives designed to tackle it, they continue to spend great sums on or with firms which perpetuate the inequalities. It is now being argued by equal opportunity experts in Britain that, to help not only women but also ethnic minorities and the disabled, a contract compliance policy should be introduced – a proposal which has the support of the Labour Party.

The changes I have outlined should give women greater support at work. But a large number of women are dependent on state benefits either through their inability to find employment or through their childcare responsibilities and it is worth considering how the recent Social Security Act will affect them.

First of all, it is important to recognise the true purpose of a social security system and to understand how those early social reformers acknowledged that the role of social security went wider than just the relief of poverty. They believed that through providing collective insurance against risk and enabling a transfer of resources, both between generations and from those without dependants to those with, a social security system should also be aiming to prevent poverty. However, today, with the rise in poverty among groups such as families with an unemployed head of the household, those headed by a single parent and old age pensioners, all of which are on the increase, this objective has failed. The single aim of social security is now to keep the poorest just above the bread line.

The 1986 Social Security Act will affect women in many ways. Death and maternity grants are to be abolished in their present form and replaced by cash limited payments from the new Social Fund, paid on a discretionary basis. The very young will suffer under this system, for the limitation of help to those on income support and family credit means that mothers under 16 will get no help with maternity costs at all. Fortunately, there are very few schoolgirl mothers, but those there are tend to need more rather than less support to help them with their babies.

The widow's allowance as we have known it will be abolished and replaced by a lump sum of £1000 on bereavement. Rights for maternity allowance will be limited to claimants with recent work records and it is anticipated that up to 94,000 mothers will lose their right to this when the new qualification test is applied.

Although many of the other changes are not specifically

directed towards women, they too will suffer from withdrawal of single payments for furniture and other needs, the requirement of supplementary benefit claimants to pay a 20 per cent proportion of their rates, the £250 million cut from housing benefits and the replacement of family income supplement with family credit, a means-tested top-up for families on low wages.

Concern was expressed from all parties in Parliament about how these changes would affect some of the vulnerable members of our society. In particular, I regarded the clause restricting the right to free school meals as very damaging for poor families, and introduced an amendment to counter this measure during the passage of the Bill through the House of Lords. Under the previous system the local education authorities had had a statutory duty to provide school meals and milk, free of charge, to the children of parents on supplementary benefit and/or family income supplement. Certain additional children who were needy also benefited from a local authority discretionary scheme for low-income families. However, the new regulations required local education authorities providing school meals and milk to charge for them in all cases except those where parents were to receive the benefit replacing supplementary benefit, i.e. income support. This meant that 545,000 children would lose their right to free meals and that their parents would receive a cash compensation of £2.20 a week instead.

I visited several primary schools in the inner London area to see for myself how this system would work. I best remember one in Lambeth. The head teacher, a Frenchwoman with enormous warmth and a total commitment to small children, told me of the conditions of life in the housing estate from which most of her children came. The families living there were devastated by unemployment and poverty, with the mothers stretched to the limit in their efforts to make ends meet. By way of an example she told me of the mother who each Thursday borrowed two pounds to tide her over until her next Giro cheque. She would buy bread and potatoes, and then, as soon as she could, return the money. The head teacher kept the £2 in her desk and each week the money wended its way backwards and forwards between her and the mother until it really became unclear whose money it was.

The same teacher told me how approximately 80 per cent of the children at her school were on free meals and that most of them would lose this benefit with the new regulations. When I asked her if some of the mothers might in fact prefer the cash compensation to help with the budget she looked at me aghast. 'People with so little money can't budget. They're always in debt. Any cash they have in the house just goes; it goes to stop the gas being turned off, to buy a pair of shoes without which a child cannot go to school, or to a bullying husband wanting to go to the pub, and so on. Even with the best intentions, the poorest mothers will never manage to put the school meal money aside each week and then we'll get the children coming to school without a penny. And what will we do then? Turn them away or give them a meal and hope the money will eventually turn up?'

Pointing to a little girl sitting close to us she said, 'Do you see the way she is eating; piling her spoon as full as she possibly can and opening her mouth very, very wide? She's desperately hungry; eating like that is a sign of it. She probably hasn't had anything since lunch yesterday and I've noticed that when she arrives at school after the weekend she looks sort of shrunken. We know now that the school dinner is such an important source of nutrition to children from the poorest families; that's why the school meal service has worked so hard recently to improve its quality.'

On the day of the debate I moved my amendment with all the persuasion at my command, the head teacher's warning still ringing in my ears. I said that the only way to benefit deprived children and to help mothers under pressure was to provide the school dinner in kind rather than cash. I told them of the survey among mothers carried out by the Child Poverty Action Group which showed that eight out of ten mothers questioned wished to continue with the dinner in kind rather than the cash substitute, even if the compensation was at an even higher level than the one offered.

I was given support from every side of a packed House but, unfortunately, many of the peers present were in London to attend a Buckingham Palace garden party. Their chauffeur-driven Rolls-Royces were waiting outside to take them on. They were not the type to feel sufficient concern for free school meals to vote against their own party. So, in this ironic fashion, we lost the day to the Government who, supported by the beautifully attired tail-coated peers, defeated our amendment by a substantial majority. Watching them filing through the lobbies opposing the reinstatement of the meals contrasted so cruelly with my vision of the small child at Lambeth, eyes intent on her plate, devouring the food.

We did win the arguments, however, a fact which was recognised by the Labour leadership who, a week later, gave a commitment to reinstate the lost free school meals and to allow local authorities to provide discretionary schemes.

A Labour Government's first objective will be to take as many people as possible out of social security and into employment, but it will also review urgently the new Act with a view to making good the losses suffered by the poorest.

Housing

It has been my intention in this essay to focus on the key components which make up the lives of women today and examine some instances where their needs differ from those of men. With this and the fact that women spend a great deal of time in their homes in mind, it seems relevant to include some reference to housing policies. For most women home is not simply a place of rest and refuge, it is where they spend a great deal of their time and where the greater part of their children's upbringing takes place. The kind of house they occupy is thus central to their lives and has a strong influence on their health and well-being.

Before specifying what housing difficulties women experience and the remedies a Labour Government would introduce, I would like to highlight some aspects of the present Government's housing policy. First and foremost it must be stated how in general terms these policies have brought about an entirely negative situation whereby, on the one hand, there are hundreds of thousands of unemployed construction workers and, on the other, a deteriorating and insufficient housing stock combined with a growing number of homeless people. A programme of house construction would not only remedy this paradoxical situation but also be one of the best means of reflating the economy in a way which is both labour intensive and import resistant. The urgency of putting the preparations for such a programme into effect is growing as cuts in apprenticeship and training opportunities lead to a shortage of skilled labour. A Labour Government would therefore need to act swiftly to reverse this position by providing the necessary training programmes.

There is little doubt that homelessness has greatly increased. It is estimated that, for the first time, the number of households officially accepted as homeless has now exceeded 100,000. Of this figure 95 per cent come from those people within the priority categories, meaning that many others, in particular childless women, fall outside the net. Many of those who have a statutory right to be housed by local authorities are families with children, often lone mothers, who while waiting to be housed are placed in bed and breakfast accommodation where they often remain for many months. There seems no better way of describing the plight of these families than by quoting an extract from a speech I made in the House of Lords on the subject of homelessness nearly three years ago, since which time I fear the situation has only worsened.

In introducing the debate, I pointed out that the reason so many people were without homes was that the only accommodation available was too expensive. I described my visit to a bed and breakfast establishment in Earl's Court where I had been invited by a 22-year-old Jamaican girl called Yvonne. The House listened attentively as I told her story.

'. . . Yvonne, her husband and their six-month-old baby

had already spent eight months there. They had been obliged to leave their private rented home in Camden when the baby was due, since their contract there disallowed young children. The Camden authority responsible for finding them a house, but unable to do so, placed them as far away as Earl's Court in this accommodation for which they paid over £100 a week, with Yvonne and her husband, who was in work, contributing £16. The room was obviously designed for a very short-term occupancy. It was only just big enough to hold the baby's cot, one chair, a small table, a small cupboard and a single bed. The couple had removed the other single bed to provide a minuscule amount of space. There were washing facilities, but if Yvonne wished to do any cooking she had to share the single gas cooker in the basement with anywhere between 17 and 25 other families, all with children of under five years of age. She said she occasionally cooked very early in the morning but that usually they lived off take-away food which they ate sitting on the bed and the one chair. There were no communal laundry facilities or fridges.

'With great fortitude Yvonne said there were worse places than this and how it was worst for parents – in many cases single parents – with older children. Cooped up in restricted areas, having previously lost friends and homes, and with their education disrupted, children often showed signs of either serious withdrawal or disruptive behaviour. She described how many of these lone mothers spent months and months in temporary accommodation, some awaiting the result of divorce proceedings, others having left their homes because of domestic violence and found themselves in a state of limbo. She told me of the women with children in care who found themselves trapped in a Catch-22 situation whereby they were unable to acquire permanent accommodation through having no dependent children with them, and were equally unable to get the care order lifted because they had no decent place to live. She spoke of the nervous strain that many of the women were under, how their health was often affected and how so many family relations suffered . . .'

I believe this description accurately reflects the unbearable pressure women and their children undergo when they are accommodated in this fashion and throws light on the absurdity of a housing policy which permits it. This all points to the urgent and basic need for a programme of house construction. The Association of Metropolitan Authorities has estimated that the backlog of investment required to deal with public and private sector disrepair and for new building amounts to £75 billion – £7.5 billion a year over a ten-year period. Yet local authorities, who must be the best placed to assess the needs of those they serve, have suffered not only from a 40 per cent cut in real terms in the central government housing budget, but have also been limited to spending only 20 per cent of the proceeds of council house sales. This is despite the fact that one of the arguments put forward by the Government to justify these excessive sales was that the funds raised would enable local authorities to invest in new buildings and repairs.

Here it must be stressed that the Labour Party is not, and has never been, unequivocally opposed to people buying their homes. What it does oppose is the present Government's obsession with promoting this particular form of tenure, rather than addressing itself to a policy which seeks to meet the whole range of housing needs. The 'Right to Buy' alone will not resolve the housing difficulties of low-paid women or single parents on social security who cannot afford to buy. To offer them the low rent accommodation they need, a Labour Government will expand investment in housing, involving funds acquired from council house sales to provide replacement units for rent. Moreover, savings in payments made to bed and breakfast hotels – estimated in 1985 to be £70 million – would also be channelled into building new houses and repairing the present stock.

A further source of funding could come from adjusting the way tax relief on mortgage interest payments currently operates. It is difficult to justify in its present form. For example, whereas in 1979/80 mortgage tax relief amounted to £1.5 billion – an amount almost exactly the same as the exchequer subsidy for local authority housing – it has now risen to £4.5 billion. Meanwhile subsidy to local authorities has dwindled to less than half a billion. In order to correct the balance, Labour would end the payment of tax relief on mortgage interest at the higher rate of tax and work towards a more equitable scheme with a greater concentration of money directed towards those most in need.

These changes should increase the extent of accommodation local authorities would be in a position to offer poorer tenants. But, at the same time, a Labour Government would strengthen the Homeless Persons Act with the intention, over its lifetime, to introduce a right to housing for *all* homeless persons. Greater attention will be given to the increasing number of women rendered homeless as a result of marital breakdown and there will be support for the magnificent work already carried out by many of our women's refuges. Family break-up, violence and sexual abuse force many women to leave home abruptly and there is a desperate shortage of emergency accommodation to cover such crises.

Houses in Multiple Occupation (HMOs) provide the worst accommodation of all and legislation to improve this situation will be introduced. Under the Housing Rights Act, measures to afford greater protection against harassment will also be provided. This is a regular feature in much of the private sector, and most usually suffered by young women.

The majority of old age pensioners are women, and as with single-parent families and young people who leave home, their numbers are rising. Thus the demand for housing is changing, with a growing need for single unit accommodation. Old people feel the cold, and deaths from hypothermia each winter are a national shame. The Labour Party would give the elderly higher heating allowances in the cold periods and provide increased support for draught proofing and home insulation services.

Finally, what are a woman's particular housing needs at the present time? First, women are more dependent on public sector housing on account of their lower earning capacity and prime responsibility as carers of children and dependent relatives. Next, women are vulnerable to physical attack, both within and outside the home. The allocation of houses and the quality of estate maintenance have a direct bearing on women's safety and physical and psychological well-being. Consequently women should have a greater say in the sort of homes they live in: the placement of lighting, routes of public paths and the durability and design of door locks are of fundamental importance. It is estimated that about 250,000 of the home accidents involving children are due to architectural features of homes. To remedy this, more women should be encouraged to work in the development and design of housing.

These, and many others, are the housing difficulties which confront women. In setting up its comprehensive housing policies a Labour Government would certainly take into account the needs and wishes of women in their own right. But in order to make their voices better heard, women themselves should be more strongly represented on the decision-making bodies: there should be more women councillors, more women on housing association management committees, and more women involved in housing allocation. And to make these changes a reality, women must be prepared to insist on them. Men, for their part, must be more willing to concede some places to women. While it is the responsibility of Government to strengthen the whole framework enabling women to achieve greater security.

Health

I have described housing issues as they relate to women at great length because I believe deeply that if a family can achieve that fundamental right, a decent home, then some of the pressures leading to divorce, juvenile delinquency, ill health, and so on, might be avoided. It is equally important, however, to comment on another all-important component in a woman's life, namely her health. And here I am convinced that the overall aim must be seen as the positive promotion of good health rather than the cure or prevention of ill health.

We know that ill health is all too often caused by poverty and bad housing, by stress in the home and workplace. Any serious commitment to improving women's health must therefore involve attention to all the facets of their lives which contribute to ill health. Despite the fact that women live longer than men, they experience a heavier burden of both chronic and acute illness during their life-time. On the one hand, this high incidence is likely to be related to the isolation of bringing up children; on the other, it may be related to the stress and fatigue resulting from attempts to reconcile the conflicting demands of home and workplace.

Contrary to popular opinion, stress is commonly associated with jobs typically performed by women, jobs which are monotonous, physically exhausting, time pressured, allowing no control, low-paid and with little or no opportunity for advancement. Frequently women's jobs involve the handling of unpleasant substances and over-exposure to equipment such as visual display units, badly designed lighting and seating, etc.

Sexual harassment in the workplace is also a continual problem for women. A couple of years ago I visited a GLC project designed to train women as motor mechanics. The girls – many of whom came from the ethnic minorities – looked neat and efficient in their dark blue dungarees. Moreover, they were quick to learn and competent; their small and deft hands often found their way more easily than a man's through the complex machinery. But when I asked them if they would take jobs somewhere in the motor trade afterwards they looked doubtful. 'It may not be worth the hassle,' one said. 'All those catcalls and silly jokes from the men would be too much to bear.'

Labour will expand and strengthen the Health and Safety Commission Inspectorate. This will include an increase of 50 per cent in the number of inspectors and a commitment to recruit more women. There will be tougher penalties for those who break the law. Moreover, it will remove the immunity of Crown employers from prosecution and thus affect many key areas of employment, including the National Health Service itself. It will provide prompt and fair compensation for victims of accidents and ill health in connection with work and provide new rights for employment and safety representatives. These will include the right to refuse dangerous work, to be made aware of the hazards in the workplace and to suspend work where there is an imminent risk of serious injury.

Clearly health education plays a major role in preventive medicine. Labour plans to promote health education in the workplace and also to encourage local authorities to set up 'shop-front' advice and complaint services, while at the same time increasing support for environmental health services.

Central to Labour's policy for promoting good health among women will be the provision of well women centres and screening for cervical and breast cancer. In a recent survey by *Cosmopolitan* magazine, one of the three issues deemed most important by women was the allocation of sufficient money for an efficient national programme of screening for cervical and breast cancer.

At the present time over 2000 women die each year from cervical cancer, in spite of the fact that, if detected at the pre-cancer stage, virtually all these lives could be saved. The crucial necessity of screening is proved by the fact that, of those who die, over three-quarters have never had smear tests and, of those who have, some die because of defective screening methods. What is wrong at present is that many women, often those at highest risk, receive no initial call for screening. Out of 192 health authorities in England, only thirteen operate computerised call and recall cervical cytology schemes, in spite of the fact that such a scheme was recommended as early as 1981 by the Government's own Committee on Gynaecological Cytology.

Breast cancer carries an even higher death toll, and yet it is thought that out of the 14,000 who die each year, as many as 3000 could be saved by effective screening. When you translate this into human terms and think of all those families so cruelly deprived of a mother, wife or daughter, the necessity for each health authority to provide a breast screening diagnosis and treatment service which meets the national technical and organisational standards is brought home.

The Labour Party is committed to providing this service which will initially cover all women over fifty, but will be extended to lower age groups as technical effectiveness improves. It will also ensure that a properly resourced national cervical screening programme, with computerised call and recall systems, is set up in all health districts to cover every woman at risk. All women will have the right to a cervical smear test every three years and extra funds will be set aside for research and for appropriate laboratory facilities for smear testing. To provide a safety net for those women unwilling to go to their doctors or to the clinics, support will be given for mobile screening facilities, with women doctors, to be made available in shopping centres and housing estates as well as in the workplace. And to encourage women to go for screening on a regular basis, they will be able to do this in paid time. As Chairman of the Women's National Cancer Control Campaign until last year, I learnt how invaluable was the medical support and relief from anxiety provided by advice services and mobile clinics. The telephone in the office went continuously with worried voices seeking reassurance about new symptoms. And while women may often refuse to go to their GPs for tests – in case it looks as if they are 'making a fuss' – they will happily queue outside a mobile clinic chatting with their friends.

In spite of the crucial role played by well women centres, at least 93 health authorities do not have such a service. The ethos of these centres is to encourage women to take control of their own bodies and responsibility for their own health. The Labour Party believes that every health authority must provide such a centre, each made up of a paid full-time coordinator and at least one female counselling session and GP surgery each week, with precise information available regarding screening, contraception, maternity, infertility and abortion services as well as social welfare benefits.

Statistics show that women are catching up with men when it comes to lung cancer, heart disease and liver cirrhosis. There has been an appalling lack of research on women's smoking and drinking habits and the ways in which women could be encouraged to give them up. Much of the anti-smoking and anti-drinking campaigning for women has been aimed at pregnant women, with the implication that women's health only becomes important when they are having babies. Yet there are reasons why women are drinking and smoking more. For instance, they may feel it helps to reduce the tiredness, stress and isolation which result from trying to combine a working life with domestic responsibilities or coping with children on a low income.

The Labour Party would take certain measures to protect women from this health risk. It would ensure greater controls on alcohol advertising, and prohibit the advertising of tobacco except at point of sale. It would also campaign to draw attention to the ill effects of smoking and alcohol misuse and provide more support for NHS facilities and to voluntary organisations to encourage people to stop smoking and help those with alcohol problems.

There are so many other areas which govern women's health to which I would like to refer. However, there is one central aspect which influences all those areas – namely, the necessity for women to be given more say and real involvement in the provision of general medical services. There need to be more women on community health councils, regional and district health authorities and family practitioner committees, as well as in the profession itself. The Labour Party would give active encouragement to this as well as providing hospital facilities run solely by women for women.

Women in Northern Ireland

My personal interest in Northern Ireland leads me to add a few words about the women in the Province whose lives are affected by the particular social, economic and political conditions which prevail there. It should also be said that attitudes there tend to favour the role women have traditionally held in the home and the concept of women being given the right of a wider choice is less developed. There is a multiplicity of reasons for this, the major ones being strong social pressure and the fact that Northern Irish families, both Protestant and Catholic, are larger, making it harder for the women to combine the dual role of mother and worker. Moreover, the job opportunities are few as the level of unemployment in the Province, at present standing at 22 per cent, has always been higher than in the rest of the United Kingdom.

Although childcare services are insufficient on the mainland of Britain, the situation is much worse in Northern Ireland. There are no state nursery schools at all, although children of four years old can be taken into primary schools. However, working mothers in Northern Ireland do have one important advantage, and that is the greater cohesion of the extended family. Women going out to work will very often leave their child or children with a relative on a fairly permanent basis.

One major disadvantage with which Northern Irish women have to contend, however – and this cannot be over-emphasised – is a higher degree of poverty and deprivation. Indeed, they are overwhelmed by poverty. The reason for this comes from the cumulative effect of bigger families, higher unemployment, lower wages, higher heating costs, poorer housing (although the present increased housing programme promises eventually to bring the level up to the UK average) and higher anxiety and stress arising out of the violence in their society.

I think I can probably do no better in completing this sketch of the lives of women in Northern Ireland than by describing two women's projects I visited in January 1987. In each case the project leaders had sent details of their scheme to be considered by the panel of judges for the Christopher Ewart-Biggs Community Prize, a prize I set up about three years ago to complement the Memorial Literary Prize which for the last ten years has been awarded to writers contributing through their work to the creation of better understanding between the people of Ireland and Britain. The Community prize was designed to reward those working at community level in Northern Ireland in the field of reconciliation and with social problems brought on by extreme poverty and the presence of sectarianism and violence. Each year we choose a different area of activity. Thus the first year's theme was to look at projects for young people. Next came the turn of community projects designed to enrich the lives of children between the ages of five and ten. This year we will reward projects aimed at helping women living in difficult environments.

I kept my coat on when we visited the first project, the Women's Information Drop-in Centre at Ormeau Road, Belfast. The temperature was distinctly low, but the spirit and enthusiasm of the two women in charge was high. They told me of their work in helping women contend with the strain, both financial and emotional, which wives and mothers in that socially deprived area of South Belfast endured. They estimated that only about one in every forty heads of household were in regular full-time employment. The objective of their Centre was to provide a 'base' for the local women, many of whom suffered from despair, depression and a general feeling of isolation. Philomena and Joyce, the leaders, felt that the Centre would provide these women with an opportunity to chat, read some magazines, have a cup of tea and benefit from the advice and support they might gain from meeting other women in the same circumstances. They hoped to encourage creative activity among the women with ideas for training and to attract young girls, some of whom were getting into all sorts of trouble, including joy-riding. (This is an extreme way in which young people in Northern Ireland demonstrate their sense of alienation. Very young boys and girls steal cars and then – for kicks – drive them through the military and police checkpoints. On many occasions this draws fire upon them with the resulting danger to their safety and lives.)

Our second project, the Ballybeen Women's Group, was

situated in an immense housing estate just outside Belfast, which housed 2500 Protestant families. Here there was a 76 per cent level of unemployment. Like the other, this project wished to offer companionship, advice and basic training to women but, on top of that, it saw itself as a pressure group. In line with all who are concerned with poverty in Northern Ireland it had taken exception to the Government's proposed changes to social security legislation. Besides carrying out information work on this issue, three women from Ballybeen were among the group who travelled to Westminster to deliver a petition to the Prime Minister.

I left Belfast that day with an awareness not only of the fundamental problems encountered by women in Northern Ireland but also with a fascinating insight into the contrasting cultures between the two communities. The two women in the Catholic community of Ormeau spoke volubly and with passion of their problems in philosophical and general terms, whereas the women of Ballybeen, neatly dressed and speaking in the level, clipped tones of the Protestant, discussed specific issues and the logical ways of dealing with them.

This visit reinforced my earlier conviction that a priority for women there is to receive help in their struggle against poverty. Nowhere in the UK would the promise of a rise in child benefit of £7.30 for the first child and £3 for each subsequent one, promised by the Labour Party, assist mothers of large families more than there. This would be equally true of the commitment to a £5-a-week rise in the single person's pension, £8 for couples, and the £2.20 one-parent family benefit also promised.

A Ministry for Women

I hope I have now said enough to show how complex are the circumstances which surround a modern woman's life, and how great the need to bring coherence to the policies affecting them. The Labour Party believes the only way of bringing about the necessary coordination is through the establishment of a Ministry for Women, to draw together all the threads representing women's interests and, from a central position, to assess their needs and formulate policies to meet those needs.

The Minister for Women would be given a seat in the Cabinet and be backed by a full Parliamentary team, political advisors and committed, senior civil servants. Although not necessarily a large Ministry, it would be high-powered, with a clear set of political priorities, and placed within the Cabinet Office. The importance of a strong personal commitment on the part of the Prime Minister to the Ministry's objectives cannot be over-emphasised and past experience in other countries has shown that unless a position close to the centre of power is held by a Ministry overlooking women's affairs then its work is rendered less effective, and its Minister isolated and marginalised.

The role of the Equal Opportunities Commission should also be strengthened. It is generally agreed that its work in promoting and informing people about equal opportunities and ensuring that employers obey the law has been of enormous importance. But in order to provide the Ministry with a strong supportive machine, the Commission should be given more teeth. Furthermore, the existing equal opportunities legislation – the Equal Pay Act and Sex Discrimination Act – are insufficient to bring about the major changes needed to provide equal opportunities for women at home and at work, and should therefore be revised.

On a third count, there is little doubt that women are in no way sufficiently represented in the decision-making bodies. It would not be possible for a government to bring this change about overnight, but there is one area they can immediately influence, namely the appointments made to public bodies.

At present, the number of people appointed to the boards of nationalised industries, to quangos, and so on (i.e. those appointments for which the Government is responsible) is 34,000. Out of that number the proportion of women at the present time ranges from 3 per cent to 20 per cent over all the different areas. The objective would not be to appoint women on to these bodies purely because they are women, with no regard to ability, but the Labour Party believes that there is a great number of women both able and willing to make a contribution to the work of these public bodies while at the same time being able to oversee other women's interests.

In order to bring about this wider participation, the Ministry for Women would monitor all appointments to public bodies, establish contacts with women willing to serve on them and make nominations from those women. Arising out of this process, targets would then be set for increasing female membership after consultation with the Minister for Women and each government department.

There is little doubt that in order to bring about widespread change, it would be necessary for the Ministry for Women to maintain a close relationship with local government. Many local councils at present develop equal opportunities' employment policies for their own employees and intervene in the labour market to promote equality. Moreover local women's committees throughout the country have helped to change the employment practices of local authorities and ensured that local council services reflect the needs and interests of women. These initiatives would be supported by the Ministry for Women, and by a statutory duty placed on local councils to promote equal opportunities within the council itself and in the community as a whole. To help women to participate in the running of their affairs, local authorities would be encouraged to set up women's committees and consult with local women when drawing up action plans for submission to the Ministry for Women. This would ensure that local needs were both known and respected.

The Labour Party believes that a Ministry for Women, built on the strong foundations I have described, would do a great deal towards meeting the needs of women today and achieving its own programme for women's equality.

Conclusion

Here I must return to my original theme of how society and state alike must ensure that our attitudes and laws are so fashioned as to enable every member of the community to lead a fair and positive life.

My focus having been on women, I have pointed out how it is not only by removing discrimination against women in education, training, employment opportunities and in the workplace that she will be enabled to reach her full potential, but also by supporting her with better health services, improved housing, and so on. I have traced the different stages in her life cycle, showing how as a girl she needs a happy family background and an education on a par with her male peers, enabling her to take the first steps into adult life. Then, as a young woman, she deserves to be treated by potential employers without discrimination, and to be free of sexual harassment.

When she marries, she will in 90 per cent of cases embark upon a dual role of mother and worker and will want society to recognise the demands of this role. Employment laws must ensure that motherhood is not penalised, that women earn as much as men, and that the children of working women are cared for. This is the period in her life cycle when she will need the greatest diversity of support to enable her to fulfil her dual commitment. Then, when she grows old and lives to a great age – as so many women do – society owes her a life of dignity with a decent pension, a home, and sufficient warmth to sustain her in the winter months.

Anthony Crosland's final definition of socialism, articulated the weekend before he died, could also, I believe, be applied more specifically to a modern woman's expectation of justice. It is about the pursuit of equality and the protection of freedom – in the knowledge that, until we are truly equal, we will not be truly free.

Formulating Policies for Women

Mary Stott

The Women's Liberal Federation, founded in 1886, is the oldest of the women's political associations. Women for Social Democracy (WSD), formed in 1982, is the youngest. Yet they have been working together since 1983 to hammer out a women's policy that would be acceptable to their own members, to the policy committees and national executives of their two parties, and to the membership as a whole. Meanwhile women Liberals and SDP members formulated an 'Alliance Charter for Women' in 1983 upon which present policies have been built.

In 1983 the SDP's Policy Committee called for a document on women's policy to be prepared at short notice by women members of the National Committee, policy officers and leading members of the WSD. In 1984, this document, 'Policy for Women', was approved by the party's Assembly at Buxton.

In the same year the Liberal Party Assembly at Bournemouth had a lively, sometimes heated discussion on women's involvement in the party and their place in the community. As a result, the Working Group on Women prepared a motion on the status of women which was overwhelmingly passed at the 1985 Dundee Assembly.

The small working party of leading Liberal and SDP women which emerged from these national policy decisions then set to work to prepare the document 'Freedom and Choice for Women'. This contribution is my own personal interpretation of the document, in whose drafting I played a small part, and the women of the Alliance must not be regarded as responsible for any errors or misinterpretations in this essay.

Education

Since the Education Act 1870, education in this country has been compulsory and free, for girls as well as for boys, from the age of five years. They have sat in the same classrooms – girls on one side and boys on the other – and studied the same subjects. Only at 'secondary' level were they segregated. So our foremothers probably counted upon a future in which educational opportunities would be exactly similar for girls and boys.

Admission to universities, however, proved a difficult nut to crack. By 1873 a few young women were successfully sitting for Cambridge University Tripos examinations, but Sophia Jex-Blake and her colleagues in Edinburgh abandoned, temporarily, all hope of being able to sit the medical examinations for which they had prepared. Agneta Ramsey secured a first in the classical Tripos of 1887, and Philippa Fawcett, daughter of the suffrage pioneer, Millicent Garrett Fawcett, was placed 'above the senior wrangler' in 1890 – but Cambridge did not actually award degrees to women until the 1940s. This extraordinary fact is a reminder that girls' and women's access to equal educational opportunity has never been really equal – and still is not – to that of boys and men, more because of inbuilt traditional prejudices than because of legal limitations.

In these days of rapid technological change, the need to secure equal access to every kind of technical course becomes more and more urgent. One is reminded of the founder of the Society for Promoting Employment for Women (1857) who quickly discovered that one of the obstacles to employing women as shop assistants was their 'poor arithmetic'.

The women of the Alliance parties have no doubt whatsoever that girls' educational opportunities are restricted. 'Early specialisation,' they say in 'Freedom and Choice for Women', 'is a particular trap for young girls. Education should offer both sexes a wider view. Reform of the curriculum to broaden it right through each year of secondary school, so that all pupils continue to study arts, sciences and technical subjects up to the age of 18, is essential for individuals, and is a particularly important means to achieve equal opportunities for girls.'

What the Alliance proposes is a curriculum for all young people that would include a compulsory balance between the arts and sciences. 'We see the integration of technical, vocational and academic subjects in tertiary colleges and sixth forms as the best way forward for the sixteen- to nineteen-year-old age group, building on less specialised education in secondary schools leading to the new general Certificate of Secondary Education.'

There are two points to be stressed here: 'arts subjects' does not mean, as some people seem to assume, just 'art' in the sense of painting, drawing, art appreciation, plus literature drama, dance and all the creative areas we call 'the arts'. It means also the English language, both spoken and written, history, ancient and modern, social and political, what used to be called 'civics' – information about how the society we live in works – and other fields of study sometimes lumped together under the description 'the humanities'.

Secondly, it is necessary for all human beings to be able to communicate, orally as well as in writing, to be able to spell, as well as to pronounce. In these areas boys will be just as much handicapped by being segregated in their range of 'scientific' subjects too early, as girls who are *excluded* from those scientific and technical subjects. This may be the core of the problem, but many Alliance women members feel that girls suffer from another limitation. In mixed schools, they believe, girls get less time and attention from teachers than boys, boys being more demanding. It seems to be well established that although girls have a better record than boys of 'O' level passes in all subjects, they tend to follow 'girls' subjects' for higher study. If this is so, it must reinforce the sex division of employment opportunities and tend to trap girls into lower-paid, dead-end jobs.

It certainly seems that some male teachers, including heads of schools, tend to think of girls' capacities as inferior in the technical and scientific fields. In her *Danger, Men at Work*, Rosalind Miles quotes the head of a technical studies department who said to her, in defence of not admitting girls to his courses: 'They couldn't do the work because their hands aren't big enough – nor their brains.'* That is a traditional, culturally-absorbed prejudice which the Alliance believes must be fought tooth and nail. It is as crazy as the prejudice which led nineteenth-century male academics, especially doctors, to warn women that higher education was driving them crazy. Dr R R Coleman, of Birmingham, Alabama, in 1873 thundered 'Science pronounces that the woman who studies is lost!'

Alliance education policy is based firmly on the conviction that every human being, male or female, should be given the right to learn whatever they have the innate ability to learn and that our educational system should give the fullest possible opportunity to establish this right for every pupil.

However, girls are disadvantaged not only by limited access to the curriculum, but by the shortage of female role models at school, as well as by inadequate career guidance. While women make up 77 per cent of teachers in the primary school sector, only 43 per cent of head teachers in this sector are female, so from their earliest years boys and girls both see women in the inferior jobs. It strikes many of us as extraordinary that the governors of one of the most prestigious girls' schools in the country, Roedean, should have appointed a man as head. Surely it is also discriminatory that when an all-girls school decides to take in boys, the next head is almost certain to be a man. Imagine the horror if the next person appointed to be head of Eton or Harrow were to be a woman!

It is true that one reason for the lower number of women head teachers is absence from work through childbearing and rearing. This has to be both unjust and unwise – child rearing at home must surely be a considerable asset in 'child-training' within their school. Yet the fact that women are rarely

---

*Rosalind Miles, *Danger, Men at Work* (Futura, 1983).

promoted to headships must come to be accepted by pupils of both sexes as the natural order of things. Hence, says the Alliance, 'the pattern has to be broken by deliberate strategies'.

As for career guidance, there can be little doubt that it fails to encourage girls to widen their career expectations, or that a majority leave school with no greater ambition than to do second-class, poorly paid jobs in shops, offices, factories, etc. A recent survey in the *British Journal of Sociology of Education* stated that nearly half the girls aspired to one of three occupations – nursing, hairdressing and secretarial work. It was suggested that it was *not* stereotyping at school which influenced this choice, but rather parental attitudes and patterns. But surely stimulating career guidance at school could help girls to define and explore their attitudes. It is vitally important that girls should always be supported in any interest they show in engineering or technological jobs and should never be discouraged by the warning: 'You may find it very difficult; women are not very readily accepted in a man's world.' Making a good choice at the Youth Training Scheme stage can give access to better and more diverse skill training for young women, and special women-only courses can be set up to encourage women into non-traditional jobs.

In higher education, broader degree courses in which all students would take some arts and some science subjects would help to eradicate the unnatural division of the sexes into prescribed areas of study. Special access courses should be introduced to encourage recruitment of women into non-traditional areas.

Finally, the Alliance is deeply concerned to provide educational opportunities for people who have missed out, first time round. For many reasons women, and some men, have left secondary school with no qualifications and little motivation towards further study . . . but the desire to acquire both knowledge and qualifications may come later, perhaps even after marriage and childbearing, for girls can very easily be beguiled in their teens by the notion that a job and a boyfriend are far preferable to schooling.

The Alliance believes that there should be a range of entry

and access pointed to further and higher education and training. Developments such as part-time degree courses, the Open University, Fresh Start and Fresh Horizon courses are all welcome, but they should have a special brief to coordinate educational opportunities for women who have been out of the labour market while having and bringing up their children. And the success of such initiatives will be dependent on the political will to tackle the provision of better childcare facilities. At the very minimum, grants awarded for education and training should have a childcare allowance within them.

Childcare

Childbearing and child rearing are at the heart and core of most women's life experience. That does not mean, of course, that childcare should take up the whole of a woman's fertile life – nor does it, in today's society. It does mean, however, that women's role in bearing and rearing the nation's future citizens must be properly valued and given adequate support.

The Alliance Women's Policy supports the payment of a maternity allowance, because it encourages women to give up their employment well before the estimated delivery date and to return to it without risk to their health or that of their baby. Choice as to over precisely what period the eight weeks' payment should be made is welcome, but the Government proposal to base entitlement on recent paid work and national insurance contributions is not, for it would make many women ineligible, especially at the time of their second or third births.

There is increasing support among women for the implementation of a European Community directive that paid parental leave should be allowed to fathers at the time of the wife's confinement, and also that either parent should be allowed paid leave to cover a child's sickness. An Alliance Government would, of course, implement this directive. It would also make available a small tax allowance to cover childcare costs, similar to work expenses, eligible for tax relief for those on the basic rate of tax.

A majority of mothers give up paid work while their children are small, but of the estimated 27 per cent of mothers who do go out to work while their children are still under five, many, probably most, do so because the family cannot manage without their earnings. Obviously these mothers need nursery care for their children. Since the budget of 1984, workplace crêches and nurseries – which one might well regard as the most desirable form of day care because they allow the parent close contact with the child – have been regarded as a business 'perk' with the parents being charged accordingly in their tax bill. Surely the tax régime should help parents to provide adequate nursery care, not hinder them.

Cuts in local authority nursery places have affected many parents. There is a large private sector for childcare and the Alliance does not believe that a massive extension of public sector childcare is feasible because of the immense cost involved. Nor is it necessarily desirable, for a diverse mix of public, private and non-profit-making provision offers parents a better choice. The Alliance's agreed policy, therefore, is to encourage the provision of childcare by introducing a tax incentive for parents. This will bring some childminders, at present operating in the 'informal' economy, into the formal sector and thus encourage registration.

The Alliance also regards it as important to provide training, support and emergency services for childminders. Childminding would be an honourable and highly-valued profession if proper training and pay were provided.

The actual physical care of small children is not the only problem confronting young mothers. There is the terrible isolation they face, especially in housing estates and high-rise tower blocks. Research shows that young mothers in the inner cities are the single most clinically depressed group in the community. This is one of the reasons the Alliance advocates the creation of a special building programme for single parents, often the worst affected.

Britain falls behind most European countries in providing education for the under-fives (despite the pioneering work in nursery school provision of the famous MacMillan sisters), even though it is now well established that children's educational achievement is higher when they have had pre-school experience. Money for nursery schools, playgroups and day care centres has been cut back since 1979. To rectify this, the Alliance proposes to guarantee at least one year's educational experience for every child under five.

Parental problems are not over when the children are happily settled at primary school, for even if the mother does not have paid employment outside the home, picking up the children from school can pose problems. The Alliance urges the provision of family centres in every locality, which would provide 'drop-in' centres for mothers with young children, support groups, counselling, after-school clubs, toy libraries and playgroups. Such centres could be run largely by self-help groups like the Pre-School Playgroups Association, often from existing premises. Every young mother must surely endorse the Alliance view that all health and education facilities for the under-fives should be under one roof, to save journeys for parents and to allow for greater use of the facilities.

City-dwellers seldom have much idea of the time spent by parents and especially mothers who live in the country in delivering and collecting children to and from school and their various leisure activities. Moreover, they often have worse housing, and the Alliance is committed to undertake major programmes of repair of local authority houses, estate modernisation and new house building to suit the needs and demands of families. Women need fair access to housing of all kinds, and the Alliance would ensure that they get it, including those low-earning women who want to buy on a part-ownership basis.

Other proposals from the Alliance to improve the lot of mothers at home with small children or that of childminders at home, include ensuring that local authorities have the resources to subsidise public transport, to help bridge the gap between isolated women at home and the outside world. In the same vein, community transport schemes would be helped to provide cheap reliable transport, and public transport services would be encouraged outside peak hours, to meet the needs of shoppers and people attending clinics and evening classes, as well as those of the public in 'paid' work.

Employment

The need for positive policies to improve the position of women is probably most clearly seen in the area of employment. It is often said that you cannot change long-established attitudes and customs by Act of Parliament. This is true in a sense, but legislation is usually an essential base for achieving a radical change in attitudes as well as in practice. The Alliance believes that areas of discrimination against women need to be tackled by strong and effective laws to secure equal treatment.

Women's average weekly earnings are currently less than 70 per cent of those of men. There was a temporary improvement in the average after the Equal Pay Act of 1970 came into force, but since then the proportion has been static, largely because job segregation – jobs done by women only or men only – has increased. In Britain, 45 per cent of jobs are completely sex-segregated, a situation to be deplored both in itself and also because it makes it difficult to establish equal pay for equal work, and even equal pay for work of equal value. With whom does a woman compare herself if in her trade or profession there is no man doing any comparable job? The Alliance believes that strong laws are needed to establish equal pay for work of equal value, with an enforcement agency to fight cases for individuals and groups.

The Equal Opportunities Commission (EOC) has taken up a good number of cases and has won some victories, but a depressing number of cases have been dismissed. In the case of a catering assistant who asked that her work should be evaluated in relation to that of a painter, a joiner and a thermal engineer, leave to appeal was granted. This is the sort of comparison in which it is essential for women to seek a judgement. The overall work situation for women will not improve significantly until many such cases are won.

Among the EOC's successes was the case of twenty-two women machinists at a furniture factory. The women's claim was that their work was of equal value to that of male upholsterers. The Industrial Tribunal upheld their claim and unanimously awarded the women equal pay and an enhanced bonus allowance which would increase their weekly pay by 13.5 per cent.

Even more difficult to tackle than equal pay is indirect discrimination. It is not necessary for an employer to defy the Sex Discrimination Act by stating outright that he prefers to employ, or to promote, a man. When he decides that he prefers the qualifications and experience of candidate A to the qualifications and experience of candidate B, he does not need to reveal to anyone, and may not fully appreciate himself, that the qualification that really makes him prefer candidate A is that he is male.

The Alliance believes that government, both national and local, should take the lead in implementing an equal opportunity policy in employment. All government departments, public authorities and nationalised industries should have to submit statements of their equal opportunities policies to the Human Rights Commission, which an Alliance Government would establish. An Alliance Government would, of course, see that its own practices did not discriminate against either sex and would grant public contracts only to employers who had adopted, and were adhering to, equal opportunities policies. To achieve equal opportunity status, employers would have to monitor the progress of women and examine all their employment procedures to eliminate sex discrimination.

An important aspect of the Alliance women's policy is concerned with part-time employment. There are currently four million female part-time employees as against only half a million male part-time employees in Great Britain. Part-timers make up about 20 per cent of the workforce, a figure expected to rise to 25 per cent with the advent of new technology, especially in office work, and the growing popularity of part-time hours with employers.

Regularising and improving the conditions of part-time employment is an urgent necessity. It is obvious that new technologies are decreasing the number of hours' labour required in factories, offices and businesses of all kinds to provide the nation with the goods and services it needs. Moreover, the pattern of family life is changing in favour of more time spent in the home by men as well as women. Adequately paid and regulated part-time work would enable all women who wished it to secure a greater degree of economic independence while their children were still young, and fathers to have a more rounded life, with more time spent with their families.

At present part-time work is characterised by low pay, poor promotion prospects and few training opportunities. Part-time workers often have no rights to sick and holiday pay and few have access to pension schemes. Eighty per cent of part-time work is in the low-paid service sector. Some part-time workers face great insecurity due to lack of enforceable contracts and employment protection. Few belong to trade unions and, when they do, their interests often come a poor second to those of full-time workers, who tend to be predominantly male. Part-time workers who earn less than the lowest national insurance threshold (£39 a week at the time of writing) are not entitled to employment benefit or an old age pension in their own right. The national insurance contribution system thus encourages employers to pay wages below this threshold.

Believing that all these disadvantages of part-time work are unfair, the Alliance supports the European Community's draft directive to equalise the status of part-time work with the same benefits as full-time work, on a pro rata basis. It believes that as part-time work expands in response to a more widespread use of new technology, an improvement in conditions will benefit both sexes, and that the extra immediate cost to employers would very soon be outweighed by the benefits of employing part-timers on a larger scale. There is considerable evidence that part-time workers achieve a higher productivity and a lower absentee rate than full-time workers. Large firms, in a submission to the House of Lords Select Committee on the European Community's draft directive, indicated that the costs to them of extending all rights to part-timers in proportion to hours worked would be minimal.

The Alliance is also concerned about the running down of the Wages Council Inspectorate. The councils currently look after about 2.7 million workers, four-fifths of whom are women, mostly in the service industries. The Low Pay Unit recently estimated that 8.25 million workers earn less than £115 a week, approximately two-thirds of average male earnings, and that two-thirds of those workers are women. Just under one million earn £80 a week, of whom three-quarters are women. There is considerable evidence that the under-payment of Wages Council minimum rates has a high incidence for part-time work. Under-payment has increased considerably since 1979 and latest figures suggest that 41% of firms are underpaying illegally, compared with 31 per cent in 1979.

There is a strong need to safeguard the protection of home workers, whose numbers are growing and will almost certainly continue to grow, as new technologies make work at home feasible for a wider range of jobs. Such women rarely have entitlements to sickness, holiday or redundancy pay or any pension rights. Yet they save employers rent, rates and power expenses, and some home-based jobs depend on use of the individual's own car and/or telephone for which they are paid minimal expenses.

The Alliance urges that minimum rates of pay should be established for home work and that there should be an increased number of inspectors to enforce them. At present home workers are nearly all people who have responsibilities for members of their family – children or elderly relatives – which keep them at home.

Health

Women are the major consumers of health care – not because their constitutions are less strong than those of men, but because of the special needs connected with childbearing and the fact that more of them survive into really old age. Women usually have more contact with the family doctor, partly because they usually escort their children to the surgery, but chiefly because, during their fertile years, they need to consult a doctor about contraception as well as pregnancy and delivery.

Half a century ago the troubles associated with the menopause may have been exaggerated, as perhaps difficulties associated with pre-menstrual tension may have been later. Nowadays very few women complain about the effects of 'the change of life', but difficulties and disturbing experiences do occur, and the sufferers often find it difficult to discuss them with a male doctor.

It seems perfectly natural that most women – one survey recently suggested it was 95 per cent – would greatly prefer to consult a woman doctor about gynaecological and obstetric matters. Indeed, for many ethnic minorities, access to a woman doctor is vital. Yet only 15 per cent of the principals of medical practices are women. Even more surprisingly, only 13 per cent of gynaecologists are women; yet how deeply women care about having access to a well-trained and sympathetic woman doctor became very clear from the massive support accorded to Mrs Wendy Savage when she was suspended from her consultancy at the London Hospital.

The Alliance believes that if patients are to have the right – as they should – to choose a woman doctor, the Royal Colleges must change their training practices and make it possible for women to take part-time training posts during the years when they have young children themselves.

Probably the greatest fear for most women in the sphere of health is of developing cancer, yet the availability of cancer screening is by no means satisfactory. GPs are only paid to provide cervical cancer tests for women over 35, or for those who have three or more children. Very few doctors send out notices to encourage high-risk women to come for tests. Laboratories carrying out such tests are now so hard pressed that results are often not available for as much as six weeks. There is evidence that in some areas tests are badly conducted and that women may fail to be informed of the results, which renders the test virtually useless.

Premature deaths from breast cancer are far higher than those from cervical cancer, yet many of these could be avoided if proper preventive action were taken. Nationwide screening programmes should be introduced for all women.

In the last few years self-help groups have sprung up, many led by women, which have identified gaps in health care provision. Many are concerned with better health education and preventive medicine, both of which have been particularly affected by cuts in health service funding. The Alliance is totally committed to a free health service, but it is anxious that resources should be made available more efficiently, especially to women. We should commit ourselves to establishing well women clinics, and encourage them to call in patients by advertising and by mailing. The clinics could be part of a medical centre in a local hospital, or take the form of special sessions at an already established medical facility.

Bringing together these services and making them extensively known would be a major contribution to the Alliance policy of shifting resources within the National Health Service towards preventive medicine. Services offered would include ante- and post-natal care, infertility treatment, cancer screening, rape counselling, marriage guidance and drug addiction guidance, particularly that relating to tranquilliser abuse. The demand for the latter has increased for, as is well known, isolated women at home tend increasingly to suffer from depression and, all too often, are being treated by the prescription of tranquillisers. Quite large numbers of women have become addicted and need help to give up the pills. In addition, they need help in order to change their lives to lessen and get rid of the depression.

The Alliance advocates free contraception for men and women of all ages, to be provided in confidence. Those under sixteen should be encouraged to tell their parents, but we believe it should be made plain to all young people that they have a right to confidentiality. Prevention of unwanted teenage pregnancies should be given a high priority. It is the Alliance view that although abortion is a matter of conscience on which members of both the SDP and the Liberal Party have strong views and must be allowed the right to express them fully and freely, the Government should have the responsibility to administer and sustain existing legislation fairly and justly. It would therefore ensure that all women, wherever they may live in Britain, have the right to obtain abortions under the National Health Service, under the Abortion Act of 1967, while giving all doctors and nurses the right to withdraw from such services on grounds of conscience.

The infertile deserve positive aid to an equal extent. It is said that at least one in ten families in Great Britain suffers the pain of being unable to have children. The development of *in vitro* fertilisation gives such families real hope. Some fear the possible dangers of the embryo research which has led to *in vitro* fertilisation, and the Alliance strongly supports the recommendation of the Warnock Committee to set up a licensing body to ensure strict limits to such research. *In vitro* treatment is at present available only in some parts of the country. We believe that it should be extended within the NHS so that all infertile women who might benefit would have access to it.

Taxation and Benefits

Many married women have been accustomed to leave income tax matters to their husbands or, if they are wage earning, to their employers, accepting their PAYE deductions without question. But in these days of massive employment of married women, their greater financial independence and increased awareness of deductions, allowances and benefits, unease has been growing steadily, notably among women's organisations of all types, as to whether our present tax system is fair and reasonable as far as women are concerned.

Outstanding among all the criticisms of the system is that in the last resort a husband is still responsible for his wife's tax. Section 37 of the Income and Corporation Taxes Act of 1970 states specifically that 'a woman's income shall be deemed to be his [her husband's] income and not her income'. This means that it is Denis Thatcher, not Margaret Thatcher, who is finally responsible for the income tax of the present Prime Minister and First Lord of the Treasury! One cannot help wondering how a woman of Mrs Thatcher's strong and independent character can tolerate such an indignity.

There is increasing support, too, for the view that every citizen should be assessed and taxed separately, as an individual. This would not be entirely fair, however, if by individual assessment and taxation those married couples who are well off are able to transfer unearned income from one spouse to the other. For this reason, the Alliance, while committing itself to separate taxation, believes that unearned income over £500 a year should be jointly taxed.

The complicated area of tax is full of pitfalls for those who believe radical change is necessary. Most of our tax and benefit system is still operated on the assumption that in every household the man is the breadwinner and that his wife, like his children, is his dependant. Yet a majority of women now work outside the home for most of their married life; 70 per cent of married women with dependent children over the age of ten are in paid employment.

Increasingly, therefore, there is a feeling that the married man's allowance, given irrespective of whether his wife is working or not, or whether they have dependent children, is out of date. The Alliance believes that the married man's allowance should be abolished (while protecting pensioners from the effects of this change) and that the saving should be used to increase child benefit in real terms for families with only one earner.

The Alliance opposes the Government's proposal to give each spouse a personal tax allowance transferable to the other spouse, fearing that this would encourage men to prevent their wives from seeking work because their own incomes would fall when their wives returned to paid employment.

Another discriminatory tax allowance is the additional personal allowance for those bringing up children without a partner. It is available to married men with children and to a totally incapacitated wife, but not to women in the same position.

Under the present system, either partner has the right to claim the joint supplementary benefit. In practice, this is usually collected by the man, who may or may not pass the money on to his family.

Both our taxation and social security system still operate under the outdated assumption that, on marriage, every woman automatically becomes responsible for all child and household care. Only recently was there a change in the regulations affecting claims for housewife's non-contributory benefit. Previously every housewife had to fill in a detailed questionnaire to establish her actual degree of incapacity, asking, for instance, whether she could clean her floors, dust, do the washing and/or the shopping, etc., and a pension was only granted if the tasks listed could not be performed adequately. Now a certified 80 per cent incapacity will establish the invalidity pension – surely the direction in which any policy for women would aim to proceed.

An even more painful result of the assumption that a woman at home is to be regarded as the dependent of 'the man of the house' is the attitude towards widows' pensions and supplementary benefit awarded to single mothers. If any such woman is thought to be receiving regular visits from a man, or takes in a lodger to help to make ends meet, the assumption is often made by social security officials that he is cohabiting, and therefore must be financially responsible for her. The National Association of Widows has fought many cases at tribunals when widows' pension books have been withdrawn by a visiting official on suspicion of cohabitation. Apparently this practice is less common today in the case of widows but, if anything, is increasing in the case of women on supplementary benefit. Surely this is the only instance under British law where a person is assumed to be guilty before any investigation or enquiry? Alliance policy, of course, is to end the practice.

The Alliance also proposes to integrate employees' national insurance contributions with income tax, at the same time compensating pensioners. This reform would benefit millions of women, because they form the bulk of low-paid workers.

It would also divide equally between two adult claimants their aggregated benefits, and, where there are children, pay benefits in respect of them and the household to the caring parents.

There is one other major area which needs to be addressed, namely the support for women (and men) who are going through separation or divorce. The Alliance would make legal aid much more flexible in this regard, to allow solicitors and other counsellors to give conciliation advice to the parties concerned before starting any court proceedings. Once that has happened, however, and the divorce has gone through, the Alliance would make maintenance orders enforceable by the court after a maximum of three months of arrears have built up without just excuse, and grant legal aid automatically and immediately to either spouse to bring proceedings. The Alliance would also ensure that maintenance payments are paid gross.

To achieve these ends, and to ensure that the whole painful area of divorce and separation is handled more sensitively, the various parts of the judicial system which deal with family matters must be brought into one family court system, conciliation services supported and extended, and women who have left the family home with children must not be deemed to have rendered themselves homeless. This housing subject is complicated and vexed, and much attention needs to be paid to it. Suffice it to say here that a woman with children who has left the family home should be treated exactly as anyone else on the waiting list for housing, according to her priority rating.

It is also vital to ensure to all married and cohabiting women an equal share in the family home, regardless of whose name the house is in, where both partners had lived there for a long time or had purchased it together as a joint home. Similarly all tenancies should be in joint names to avoid similar problems should a break-up of the marriage or relationship occur.

Of equal importance, because all these areas of tax and benefits are so complicated, and such issues as divorce and separation are so distressing, the Alliance would support and encourage the growth of advice services such as the Citizens' Advice Bureaux and the independent advice agencies, as well as law centres. Although this service would not be particularly aimed at women, but rather targeted at areas of acute social need, there is good reason to suppose that it would act particularly to women's advantage, especially over such areas as discretionary benefits.

Women and Public Life

Most people, men as well as women, are critical of the fact that there are not more women in Parliament, on local councils and in other public bodies. They are then apt to add, and this is women as well as men, 'But we must have the best person for the job, mustn't we? There don't seem to be enough able, well-qualified and experienced women around, do there?'

To this the SDP-Liberal-Alliance women will reply, 'Rubbish.' In fact, in their document 'Freedom and Choice for Women' they declare: 'Women are largely disenfranchised, excluded from the corridors of power, and have little say in the decisions that are made on their behalf, often disastrously, by men.'

Is it really true that women are 'disenfranchised'? Certainly, in the sense that virtually all decisions in Parliament, in the courts and local government are taken by an overwhelming majority of men. There are only 29 women MPs out of 650 in the House of Commons. There are only 45 women life peers in the House of Lords, while there are 26 seats reserved for bishops of the Church of England, all male, and 790 for hereditary peers, similarly all male. Since the life peerage system was introduced in 1958, eight times as many men as women have been elevated to the Upper House.

The situation in local councils is similar. Only 19 per cent of women are councillors, though this is a job many women could fit in with family life. When the GLC and the Metropolitan councils were abolished in 1986, just ten women out of 220 people were considered by the Government for the residuary body, and not a single woman was appointed. 'Women still not good enough for public bodies,' was the headline given by the Equal Opportunities Commission's newsheet 'Update' to a report on this item.

And that seems precisely the view of the majority of government ministers and civil servants who are responsible for the appointment of people to a very wide range of commissions, committees, boards, research councils, advisory bodies, and so on. When the Equal Opportunities Commission analysed these appointments it produced some disturbing facts. For example, the Secretary of State for Education is responsible for 727 appointments to the various bodies under his control. Women make up just 11.8 per cent of the appointees. On sixty-five of the bodies on the Department of Education and Science (DES) list there was no woman at all and a further fifteen had only one woman member. The medical, science and social science research councils have fifty-three members between them, not a single one of whom is a woman. This lack of women at the DES is almost beyond belief, since such a large part of the nation's educational provision is in the hands of women and since one at least, the Rt Hon Margaret Thatcher MP, was thought competent enough to run the whole department as Minister for Education.

The story is the same for all government departments. According to the EOC survey, the Department of Industry could only claim 3 per cent of women among its appointees. Sometimes, as in the case of the Home Office, an apparently quite high overall percentage of women – 30.5 per cent – may conceal a serious imbalance in the most important bodies. The EOC commented: 'If the parole boards, boards of visitors, and local review bodies are excluded, the figure is reduced to 13 per cent. Of the forty-one bodies listed, fifteen have no women serving and a further eight have only one woman member.'

When women first started campaigning for better representation on these public bodies they were told that they could nominate themselves, or get their organisations or associates to nominate them, on forms supplied by the Public Appointments Unit (PAU), which would be consulted by ministers and heads of government when making appointments. This 'way in' turned out to be largely an illusion. The list continued to be added to, but also to be pruned from time to time of 'dead wood', and the appointments system continues pretty much in the same old way, with the appointment of members much like the people they are replacing – male, middle class and known personally or by repute to the minister or one or two of his trusted civil servants.

How, then, does the Alliance propose to deal with this imbalance? Firstly, of course, by encouraging women to involve themselves in political and public affairs locally, so as to get useful practical experience and to become known. It is the Alliance's view that women who have been on the committees or acted as officials of such organisations as the Women's Institute, Townswomen's Guild, the National Council of Women, the Co-operative Women's Guild, and so on, or have been actively involved in bodies such as the Business and Professional Women's Clubs or Soroptimists, in their trade unions, or even at branch level in their local political party must remind themselves that this is useful basic experience – as, indeed, is running a home. Mrs Thatcher once told a large gathering of Townswomen's Guild members, when giving a memorial lecture for Dame Margerat Corbett Ashby, that it was her experience in running a household that enabled her to make decisions so quickly.

A notable step in encouraging women to put themselves forward was taken in the autumn of 1986 by the Fawcett Society and the 300 Group, enthusiastically supported by many women Alliance members, when the Women into

Public Life campaign was launched. The conference centre at Westminster Cathedral was packed to the doors by women of all parties, allegiances and ages. It was given a good send-off by David Waddington, representing Mrs Thatcher, Jo Richardson, representing Neil Kinnock, and by David Owen and David Steel, representing the Alliance. The high spot of the day was the handing over of a bundle of more than six hundred Public Appointments Unit nomination forms, filled in by 'able and willing' women, for the consideration of the PAU's director, Geoffrey Morgan.

Alliance policy is, of course, to press ahead with bringing the names of suitable women to the attention of government departments. It also intends to recommend that an equal number of women and men be appointed to life peerages, 'pending the reform of the House of Lords, which the Alliance favours, by direct election of 50 per cent of its membership and the appointment of the other 50 per cent'. Being a new party the SDP, which only drafted its constitution in 1981, could take the bold step of requiring that every constituency party should include at least two women on every shortlist of prospective parliamentary candidates. At the time of writing there were 55 SDP and 32 Liberal prospective women candidates for the next election – an encouraging number, until one remembers that there are 650 parliamentary seats.

On the question of reserved places, or 'positive discrimination', there are mixed feelings among women as well as among men. It is argued by some that to reserve places for women degrades them by implying that they would not be appointed, or elected, on merit. It is thought that positive discrimination leads to tokenism, and that to prefer the token woman, just because she is a woman, to an experienced and able man, is obviously undesirable as well as unfair. Yet for generations men have excluded women from all kinds of jobs on account of their sex, and I cannot bring myself to believe that if one woman here or there is not quite up to the job she is inevitably worse than *any* of her male colleagues on the committee or board!

If a Minister for Women's Affairs were appointed in the

next Parliament, surely part of her job would be to examine, department by department, the nature of the quangos it appoints, and to consider which would most obviously benefit from an input of well-qualified women. She would also, surely, alert bodies such as the Women's National Commission and the Equal Opportunities Commission when vacancies were likely to arise so that women's organisations could be notified and invited to submit names.

Fair Votes

Both the SDP and the Liberal Party strongly support the need for electoral reform, believing the 'first past the post' system produces a ludicrously lop-sided result in terms of candidates elected to the House of Commons. In the 1983 General Election, 42 per cent of the electorate voted Conservative. They were represented by 397 MPs (61 per cent). Labour received 26.6 per cent of the vote and had 209 seats (32.2 per cent). Meanwhile, 25.4 per cent voted for the Alliance and were represented by only twenty-three MPs (3.5 per cent).

All very interesting, you may say, but why should proportional representation, or 'fair votes', as we prefer to call it, be included in a discussion of women's policies? There is, in fact, strong evidence to prove that women fare much better in elections in countries which have some system of proportional representation than those which do not. Two personal experiences helped to convince me that this is the case. On a visit to Dublin to make a contribution to a Focus on Women conference arranged by the Irish Women's Political Association, I kept seeing car stickers urging 'Vote for a Woman this time'. 'But I have never, never been able to vote for a woman,' I said sadly to my hosts, 'though I have voted in every general election since 1929, the first in which women voted on the same terms as men. There was never any woman standing.' (In fact, even at the last General Election in this country in 1983, there were 400 constituencies without a single woman candidate.)

Then, at about the same time as my Dublin visit, I learned that Barbara Castle, now a member of European Parliament, but then a member of the House of Commons, had said quite firmly that she was certain she would never have been elected as a Labour MP for Blackburn, Lancashire, in 1945, if it had not been a two-member seat, giving the electors the chance to vote for both a woman and a man.

Facts and figures prove that my instinctive reaction was justified. If voters have an extended choice, they will almost certainly support one female candidate. In the United Kingdom, where 51 per cent of the electorate is female, only 4 per cent of MPs are female. In Norway, 37 per cent of MPs are women, in Finland 31 per cent, in Denmark 26 per cent, in Sweden 26 per cent and in the Netherlands 18 per cent. Are we to believe the strides made by women towards equality in these countries have been so much greater than in Britain? The Scandinavian way of life is often thought to differ quite substantially from ours, and perhaps it is more acceptable for women to lead a more 'public' life there. But the incontrovertible fact is that in all these countries where women have a better representation in Parliament, some form of proportional representation is in operation.

It is disconcerting, surely, to learn that in the United States, which has a 'first past the post' system like ours, only 5.2 per cent of the members of Congress are women. Even more interesting is the situation in Australia. In the Australian Lower House women make up about 5.4 per cent of members. They are elected by the 'alternative vote' system, which is not accepted as genuine proportional representation by the experts of the Campaign for Free Votes. But in the Australian Senate, whose members are elected by the single transferable vote (as in Ireland), women make up about 20 per cent of members.

There is little or no evidence to suggest that at the next General Election in this country electors will be less willing to vote for women than for men. The immense authority the Prime Minister has achieved makes nonsense of any suggestion that by selecting a woman candidate constituency parties are lessening their chances of a victory at the polls. It is a fact that under our present voting system two-thirds of the seats never change hands at all, because a majority of electors never change their party allegiance. The conclusion one has to draw is that the local selection committee of the dominant party virtually chooses the constituency's MP.

This would be unlikely to happen if some form of fair votes were introduced but, in the meantime, women members of every political party should surely make their views known locally. The SDP has from the beginning laid down in its constitution that, in the selection of prospective parliamentary candidates, 'a minimum number of men, women and applicants who are not members of the area party in which the constituency is situated shall be included in the short list'. In practice this 'minimum number' has always been two. The Liberal Party also has a provision to ensure the presence of at least one woman on the shortlist of candidates. Both provisions constitute a very important statement of intent by the Alliance. At the time of writing the SDP has selected 55 women parliamentary candidates and the Liberals 32.

A Carers' Charter

One of the encouraging features of our times is that members of all political parties, men as well as women, are beginning to consider ways of providing support for 'the carers' in society. Twenty years ago, 'carer' was a scarcely known word. When the Rev. Mary Webster was inspired to found a small organisation to provide help for the devoted daughters of frail elderly parents, she called it the National Council for the Single Woman and Her Dependants. Now it has become the National Council for Carers and Their Dependants, reflecting a considerable change in attitudes and practices. There are now, I am sure, far more married women caring for parents and parents-in-law than single women. Other devoted carers are bachelor sons caring for senile mothers and husbands caring for an arthritic or paralysed wife. Dependants are also recognised to include young children who are mentally retarded or in some way disabled. There are certainly no fewer carers than in earlier years and it is estimated that there are now more women at home caring for the elderly than caring for young children. A Carers' Charter is thus by no means a 'women's rights' or 'equality' demand, but nevertheless it is a matter of supreme importance to women.

Some politicians take it upon themselves to lecture their fellow citizens on the duty of families to care for their ageing relations in the family home. They like to imply that 'in the old days' every elderly person made his or her home with married sons and daughters, and that it is only now, in this selfish 'permissive' society, that the demand for better provision for the old has surfaced. This is simply not true. Almost up to the Second World War the grandparents of many of today's middle-aged citizens, if they could not maintain themselves on the tiny pension then available to them, would too often be faced with the possibility of having to seek accommodation in 'the workhouse', where husbands and wives were separated into 'men's' and 'women's' wards at night and sometimes even by day.

Today only 6 per cent of pensioners live in any kind of institution. These include well-planned 'sheltered accommodation' where the residents have their own flats and bed-sits, with a resident warden to keep an eye on them, a programme of building which the Alliance would increase; 'homes for the elderly', which provide communal dining rooms and lounges and, quite often, shared bedrooms; private accommodation; or geriatric wards. Most old people continue to live in their own homes, and the rest live with their families.

The last option is always thought to be the ideal by people who have little idea of what it involves. It saves ratepayers and taxpayers quite a lot of money; it also ensures company and, usually, affection. Most families do indeed take on the responsibility of providing a home for elderly parents with the utmost goodwill but, as the years go by and the parent's dependence increases, and their mental and physical capacities deteriorate, 'caring' can sometimes deteriorate into a heart-breaking as well as a back-breaking task.

Degenerative diseases usually develop slowly. The dear mother who moves into the spare room may at first be able not only to care for herself in every way but to do several little jobs about the house, washing up, dusting, mending, stacking the dishwasher, ironing and so on. At first, though her knees are stiffening, she may be able to hoist herself in and out of the bath with a cheerful grin, with the aid of side handles and a rubber mat. A few years on she may have to be hoisted on and off the commode and hand fed, if her arthritis becomes serious.

The victim of a stroke may be paralysed down one side; the victim of Alzheimer's disease, at first endearingly vague about names and days and where to find the kettle or hairbrush, may become so 'demented' that she does not even seem to know how to fill the kettle or how to plug it in, or whether she has turned on the gas stove or lit it. In the advanced stages of Parkinson's disease the sufferer may become so crippled that he or she cannot walk across the room unaided, or be left alone in the house longer than it takes to go to the shops.

These are particularly horrifying conditions, but the majority of old people suffer some deterioration of sight, hearing and mobility. It is harder to get about, harder to keep up an interest in things, harder to avoid sinking into inertia and leaning heavily on the 'carer'. Meanwhile, the carer, of course, has other responsibilities – possibly a part-time paid job, possibly adolescent children who need patient love themselves but are not always patient with old people's quirks and oddities. Society can and surely should provide help. All of us expect to be old some day. Can we ourselves bear to think of a day when we might become an almost intolerable burden on our dear sons and daughters?

The Alliance has formulated and is promoting a Carers' Charter which, if the party comes to power, it will begin to implement locally and nationally. The first step will be to ensure that all carers, in every local authority area, will be guaranteed access to a single agency which will be responsible for all their needs and will ensure that they are getting everything available in that area. Many carers, like old people themselves, do not know where to turn and find themselves lost in a sea of bureaucracy as they tackle several departments with different requests.

The Carers' Charter makes ten provisions:
- A benefit to all those who care for the old, the sick and the handicapped at home, based on the invalid care allowance.
- Day care centres to be available for all who can make use of them, providing meals, social contact, baths, chiropody and hairdressing.
- Holiday relief for carers through the provision of places in caring institutions for short stays for the elderly and handicapped.
- Guaranteed and regular transport services to and from day centres.
- Family centres in every area.
- Meals on wheels for invalids living with a family.
- Laundry services for incontinent patients.
- Sitting services during the day and in the evening to allow housebound carers to go shopping and on outings.
- Housing priority for those requiring more accommodation in order to take in a relative who needs care, a measure which requires improved liaison between local housing departments.
- Good neighbour schemes, comprising both good neighbour and carers' self-help schemes, run where necessary by paid organisers to ensure their long-term continuation.

To help make the Carers' Charter a reality, the Alliance would aim, through its jobs programme, to increase the number of community health and personal social services workers, such as home helps.

Old Age

Any political party which does not give the most serious consideration to the problem of old age is gravely at fault. The frightening situation of many old people in the appalling winter conditions of January 1987 should have been a reminder of how inadequate much of our provision is for the care and well-being of the aged. What is far less appreciated than it should be is that a very large majority of the aged are women, so that any women's policy must take the problems of the aged into account.

According to the last Demographic Review issued by the Office of Population Censuses and Surveys in 1977, there were only 800 men to 1000 women between the ages of sixty and seventy. The ratio became 543 to 1000 between the ages of seventy-five and eighty-four, and above eighty-five there were nearly three times as many women as men. The projected figures for 1986 were not very different – a slightly higher ratio for men in the younger age groups but even lower in the over-eighties. Of these very elderly women, a very high proportion are widows, thus constituting the great majority of the 2,800,000 pensioners who live on their own.

The number of pensioners of both sexes who live in any kind of institution is not more than 6 per cent. Since the number of pensioners is estimated to reach a total of 9.5 million by 1996, and by that time the working, tax-paying population is estimated to be less than 31 million, forward planning for the care and maintenance of the aged needing support is obviously vital. As women are not only going to be the great majority of those needing care, but also the great majority of those called upon to provide it within the family, this is essentially a women's problem.

The Alliance believes that the most important thing to be tackled is poverty in old age, which it proposes to do through its integrated tax-benefit system. There are other ways of helping pensioners to cope financially, though, without driving them to apply for supplementary benefit. Their bills for gas and electricity, for example, all include a standing charge, as do the water charges. In my own area a standing charge of £12 is paid for water and £12 for sewage no matter how many persons wash, bath and flush the toilet, and how many of them are wage-earners.

Likewise, British Telecom's standing charge seems incredibly unjust. On a recent bill of my own for £42.28, the charge for 'system' was £13.95, for 'apparatus' £6.20, for VAT at 15 per cent £6.16 – a total of £26.31 – while the charge for dialled and operator-controlled calls was £20.22, only slightly more than the standing charge. The Alliance would abolish standing charges for the elderly. Personally I would go further and allow rent-free telephones for all pensioners over seventy, for the telephone is a lifeline in case of illness or accident. Many pensioners simply cannot afford the rent. One housebound 82-year-old woman of my acquaintance made up her mind belatedly that she ought to have a telephone installed, but to pay the rental she had to give up her subscription to a book club which had kept her alert and stimulated.

The Alliance estimates that 1.6 million pensioners are dependent on supplementary benefit, such as housing benefit and various single payment allowances, of whom 77 per cent are women. Their entitlement is complex and often inequitable. Many elderly persons in reasonably comfortable circumstances must have wondered why no one bothered to explain to the half-frozen lonely old widows how they should apply for that £5 weather payment when it was belatedly announced. If they had no telephone and could not safely struggle along frozen pavements, even to a pillar box, let alone to the nearest post office, how were they to make an application?

Women who do not have the necessary record of national insurance contributions and are therefore ineligible for an old age pension receive only the long-term rate of supplementary benefit. Women are far less likely than men to have occupational pensions. If they benefit from state earnings related pension (SERPS) entitlement at all they will gain very little because of their lower earnings. The Government's reform of SERPS will further depress many women's earnings-related pensions. And it should not be forgotten that there are many people now entering their eighties who retired before inflation ran riot, and whose pensions are based on a salary that by 1987 standards would be around the poverty line.

Women contributors to occupational pension schemes sometimes pay more than their male peers yet do not always receive the same benefits. Many salaried women fiercely resent the fact that a man can provide for his wife if he predeceases her, but a woman cannot provide for her husband in the event of her being the first to die. The Alliance favours portable pensions through which people can accumulate pension rights. This is particularly suited to women's pattern of employment, which is often interrupted by childbearing and rearing and may include periods of part-time work. The Alliance would extend pension rights to part-time workers on a pro rata basis.

The question of the age at which a state pension should be paid causes widespread division of opinion. Some women think it would be discriminating against women to raise the pension age. Others feel that the present system discriminates against them because it is assumed by many employers that women should be retired at sixty, whether they wish to be or not. Similarly, some men regard it as discriminatory against them that women can retire on a pension five years earlier. The Alliance policy of phasing in an equal retirement age for both men and women should be acceptable at least to a majority of men and women, so long as there is some flexibility for individuals to choose their own retirement age up to sixty-five. Some of us would prefer a flexible retirement age for both sexes from sixty to seventy, but in practice that would not be at all easy to achieve.

In this age of rapid technological change, prolonging working lives does not seem a good idea. Yet, if people are to be retired on a pension which amounts to a third or less of their wage or salary while they are still full of mental and physical energy, a great deal more thought must be given to how they, men and women alike, are to occupy their time usefully and enjoyably for the rest of their lives, and how they are to be protected against a very great fall in their standard of living.

Endpiece

Julia Neuberger

'In the cotton districts during the summer months the workers spend their evenings out of doors, more after the fashion of Continental than English towns, and on certain nights in the week anyone going into the market place can get an audience of interested and intelligent men and women, varying from 600 to 1,000 and even 1,500, who will stand for an hour or two to hear the question discussed.'*

The question was women's suffrage, the year 1905, several years before 'suffragette' was to become a household word, yet the movement was gaining ground among working-class, factory worker women in Manchester and its environs. Although there had been important women's policy campaigners in the previous century, and even earlier if one examines the work of Mary Wollstonecraft, for instance, the modern campaign for the rights of women clearly has its roots in the suffrage movement.

Much of the credit for women's suffrage goes rightly to the Pankhursts, Mrs Pankhurst having founded the Women's Social and Political Union in Manchester in 1903. The campaign of direct action was launched after the Pankhursts moved to London in 1905. Even so, it took until 1918 for women over thirty to be granted the vote, ostensibly in gratitude for what they had done during the First World War in carrying out 'men's jobs'. Universal suffrage was only achieved in 1928, at which point many women thought that

---

* Annual Report of the National Society for Women's Suffrage, 1905, as quoted in One Hand Tied Behind Us – the rise of the Women's Suffrage Movement by Jill Liddington and Jill Norris (Virago, 1978).

their goal had been reached. It is perhaps significant that the constitutional suffragists, as opposed to the militant suffragettes, believed that once women had access to the system they would be able to end all gender-based inequality and to change the male political agenda.

Before the Pankhursts, there had already been the very polite and well-behaved Manchester Suffrage Society, founded in 1867, and the Fawcett Society, with its excellent track record of campaigning for women's equality, started as the London Association for Women's Suffrage in 1866. But the national campaign really took off when John Stuart Mill failed in his attempt to amend the 1867 Reform Act to include women. The British Women's Trade Union League was founded by Emma Paterson in 1873, and Clementina Black proposed the first ever resolution on equal pay at the TUC conference in 1888. Interestingly enough, that resolution received unanimous support from male trade unionists, although cynics would argue that this was because the men were afraid that lower pay for women would threaten their own employment, since women would be cheaper to employ.

Meanwhile, what Ray Strachey called 'The Philanthropic Movement' got under way in the middle of the nineteenth century.* Louisa Twining, Mary Carpenter, Baroness Burdett-Coutts, Josephine Butler and others all involved themselves in work for the community in some respect. For Louisa Twining it was Workhouse Reform, for Mary Carpenter, Ragged Schools, whilst Baroness Burdett-Coutts contributed to almost everything, but involved herself particularly in the slums.

Florence Nightingale, an early variety of the sceptical feminist, created a proper profession for women in nursing, but gave somewhat unwilling support to the women's cause. According to Ray Strachey, 'She signed petitions and believed in women's suffrage because "it is the first principle or axiom that every householder or taxpayer should have a voice", but openly declared that she did not "expect much from it." . . .

---

* Ray Strachey, *The Cause* (G. Bell, 1928).

There is indeed a letter of hers to Harriet Martineau in which she says "I am brutally indifferent to the rights and wrongs of my sex" . . . In her absorption in her own work she judged the men and women she lived among almost wholly by their usefulness or uselessness to it.'

Josephine Butler was campaigning against the compulsory medical checks on what were described as 'common prostitutes'. Refusal to undergo these checks meant repeated terms of imprisonment, while acquiescence meant total loss of reputation at a time when a prostitute was friendless, cheerless and a 'fallen woman'. The prostitutes and brothels had been licensed by a series of items of legislation starting in 1864, referred to as 'the Acts'.

The campaign had the most enormous success, and a violent storm of opposition to 'the Acts' ensued after 1870. But it divided families and broke up friendships as people did not want to talk about such matters. It also divided the women's movement, since those who were campaigning for girls' education had to be very careful, as they saw it, about their reputations if they were to have 'young ladies' in their charge. Yet Mrs Butler caused the defeat of the likely candidate at the Colchester by-election of 1870 by speaking on the subject and a Royal Commission was set up which came round to condemning the Acts. They continued, however, as did the incredibly low age of consent of twelve (which the Commission had wanted to raise to fourteen), for another thirteen years. Mrs Butler's campaign alerted the serious thinkers to the prevailing double standards about sexual morality, but found it hard to touch the vested interests.

At the same time campaigning was also taking place for women's education, for women in the medical profession, for the right to equal pay (from time to time), and above all for the vote. The women's movement became recognisable to us in modern times with the suffragists of the late nineteenth and early twentieth centuries and their successes of 1918 and 1928 are the real beginnings of our story.

The First World War was, in a sense, a turning point in the fight for women's suffrage. It also caused an enquiry into

equal pay, a matter which was becoming increasingly significant and which was to be so much a part of the backbone of
the women's movement campaigns on both sides of the
Atlantic. Several of the original suffrage societies, notably the
Fawcett Society and the Women's Freedom League, became
general emancipation groups, and some were set up specifically for the purpose. Throughout the 1920s and 1930s MPs
were lobbied and petitioned about equal pay, public appointments and all the other remaining legal barriers to women's
equality. Yet little changed and, indeed, there were still bitter
memories of the fights over the suffrage issue, which may
well have caused some women to steer clear of the whole
matter of the further emancipation of women.

After the Second World War, however, there was no
mistaking the change in mood. Whereas women had been
given the vote and had gone home to their 'normal' domestic
occupations after the First World War, this time there was no
mass exodus from the labour market. Indeed, there are cynics
who argue that the excessive cult of domesticity and home-
making which was particularly prevalent in the USA, but also
made its mark in the UK, was deliberately engineered to force
women back into the home leaving jobs for the men. Middle-
class women had reached a plateau in their professions and
seemed unable to reach the dizzy heights. The Welfare State,
expected by some to provide automatic equality for all
classes, brought with it the expectation of equality for women
and men too. By the early 1950s Mr Justice Denning, now
Lord Denning, argued that female equality was a fact,
although he feared it marked the end of civilisation.*

The publication of Betty Friedan's The Feminist Mystique
in 1963, which touched a raw nerve and became an instant
bestseller, is often thought to mark the true beginnings of
women's liberation. Yet the fact that President Kennedy had
already set up a Commission on the Status of Women in 1962

---

* The Times, 13 May 1950, as quoted in Women's Rights at Work by Elizabeth
M. Meehan (Macmillan Education, 1985).

suggests that other things were going on as well as Betty Friedan's remarkable book. Indeed, the American women's movement really had its roots in the beginnings of support for the Equal Rights Amendment (ERA), which the Republican Party had endorsed in the 1940s, and in the Democrats' concern to find ways to improve the lot of working women.

This led ultimately to equal pay legislation in the USA, and the inclusion of women in the employment section of the Civil Rights Act. Yet the new Equal Employment Opportunities Commissioners refused to take the issue of sex discrimination seriously, and the women's movement organised itself, in considerable anger, to do battle. From that time its focus has mainly been on equal pay and sex discrimination, as well as abortion. Unlike Europe, the feminists of the late 1960s and early 1970s in the USA were not interested in specific employment protection for women, nor in the provision of childcare for working mothers. Sylvia Ann Hewlett, writing from her experience as a lecturer and top-grade economist in the USA, having grown up in Britain, argues that the American feminists were simply not interested in children. The main things on their agenda, she suggests, were abortion rights and equal pay.*

Both in the USA and, to a lesser extent, in Britain, the 1960s saw the birth of 'sexual politics'. Germaine Greer, Kate Millett, Betty Friedan herself, Erica Jong and many others started addressing themselves to the politics of women's oppression. Germaine Greer's *The Female Eunuch* became obligatory reading, as did the later *Fear of Flying* by Erica Jong. Bras were burned all over the USA and in Oxford, Cambridge and London. 'Sisterhood is powerful' became the slogan, and no one could ignore the issue. Women began to reject marriage and family structures, claiming their sexual freedom through the pill. But the link with the hippy movement and 'flower power' had worrying side-effects. In

---

* A *Lesser Life – The Myth of Women's Liberation* by Sylvia Ann Hewlett (Michael Joseph, 1987).

retrospect the sexual freedom seemed more like sexual freedom for the men, with the women being used as childbearers and sex objects, living in communes without much apparent 'sisterhood'.

Even so, the feminist philosophy began to take hold. Women's studies in universities changed from being viewed as fringe and rather amusing to being central to many courses. The 'writing out' of women from history as it was taught in schools and universities became a real issue. Theology, philosophy, literature, art and history itself were all affected. This, together with arguments about the right of women to control their own bodies (with regard to abortion as well as contraception), became the keynote of American feminism.

The impact of feminism was never quite the same in Britain, however, although there was influence from the USA in the field of legislation. Some of the trades unions acted to help women in employment. In 1963 the Shipbuilders and Engineering Workers Unions set up a committee to press for higher gradings for skilled women. In 1964, the Amalgamated Union of Engineering Workers committed itself to the idea of equal pay within a three-year period. In 1965 Ray Gunter postponed Government action on equal pay, and the TUC general secretary of the time made it clear that they would support industrial action in its favour. In 1967 a national union of women workers was formed to campaign for better treatment, and by 1968 feelings were running so high that a strike by women workers at Ford which held up £50 million worth of export orders was extremely well supported, by men as well as women. The women marched to the House of Commons, and some people argue that it was this which stirred the Government into action.

By November of 1968 Barbara Castle promised, accurately as it turned out, that equal pay would be a reality within seven years. There were more equal pay strikes around the country in 1969, and the Equal Pay Act was passed in 1970, not to be implemented until 1975. Meanwhile there were further strikes, particularly in the winter of 1973–4, which were partly or wholly about equal pay.

Barbara Castle, who had engineered a compromise between the TUC and the Confederation of British Industry (CBI) over the scope of the equal pay legislation (the TUC had been urging the adoption of Convention 110 of International Labour Organisation (ILO) on equal pay for work of equal value since 1961, and the CBI had resisted on the grounds of cost, preferring the narrower scope of the Treaty of Rome's Article 119, even though the UK was not yet part of the EEC), now argued that she was not interested in including an anti-discrimination clause in the legislation. As the Bill went through the House, the Conservative MP Robert Carr warned her that it would be ineffective without such a clause. Yet, 'although both parties were agreed about the justness of equal pay, Mr Heath's Government did little at first to rectify this omission. Indeed, in January 1972, the Home Office Minister, Richard Sharples, incurred wrath from the public galleries when he rejected Mr Hamilton's Private Members' Bill by saying that women were best suited to occupations that were extensions of their domestic roles . . .'*

Mr Hamilton tried again in 1973. This time the Bill got a second reading and went to a select committee. This seemed like a delaying tactic (an almost identical bill introduced by Baroness Seear had been sent to a select committee by the Lords), but the Government was about to change its mind. It published a consultative document in November 1973 called Equal Pay Opportunities for Men and Women. That Government then fell after the miners' strike and the new Labour Government announced its intention to legislate on women's rights.

The then Home Secretary, Roy Jenkins, and his political adviser, Anthony Lester, visited the USA to look into race and sex discrimination legislation there. As a result of their findings, there is some considerable American influence in the idea that this kind of matter can be dealt with by legislation, even though many people who supported the cause

* Meehan, op. cit., p. 66.

at the time disputed this. There was also the feeling, derived from the USA, that anti-discrimination policies do not work unless they are aimed at the effects of employment practices rather than the motives behind them. The legislation was deeply influenced by EEC thinking, too, although it can be argued that it was in fact more generous than Article 119 of the Treaty of Rome would have required at the time. Britain passed the Sex Discrimination Act in 1975 and, once again, the members of the women's movement felt that the world would change and that the 'cause' was won.

Clearly, that has by no means been the case. Britain joined the EEC in 1973, linking us to what we perceived as our more progressive European neighbours. They had been bound by Article 119 of the Treaty of Rome since 1957, although it can be argued that France had pressed for equal pay legislation out of fear that her own products would be undercut by the cheaper labour costs of other European countries.

The proportion of earnings by women as seen in relation to men's rose consistently between 1970 and 1977, with the largest jump coming before the Equal Pay Act and Sex Discrimination Act became law. By 1977, however, women had reached their peak of an all-time high on the hourly rate of 75.5 per cent of men's earnings, from which point it began to fall. Taken on a weekly basis, where men do far more overtime than women, by 1983 the figures were 62.6 per cent for manual workers and 59.9 per cent for non-manual. *Social Trends** shows pay differences between the sexes widening. In full-time work, in 1970, women earned 56 per cent of men's earnings. By 1981, this had improved to 67%. But by 1985 it was back down to 65%.

That this continuing inequality is a matter of considerable importance to all political parties is clearly reflected by the essays in this volume. Different remedies are suggested for dealing with the problem, but the fact that it is a problem is by no means denied. Yet Britain has been astonishingly slow to

---

* *Social Trends*, No. 17 (HMSO, 1987).

enact legislation, whichever government has been in power, and the very real concern of the women's organisations in all the major parties may still not be matched by action once in power.

Indeed, the single most powerful force for improvement in our legislation to protect women, specifically in the employment area, has come since our membership of the EEC. Time and again, British law has been found to be inadequate and defective by the European Court of Justice in The Hague, and measures have been necessary to strengthen our legislation, particularly in the areas of pension provision, equal pay for work of equal value, and retirement ages.

Yet though legislation has been improved – albeit sometimes unwillingly – the position of women in a variety of public organisations and trades unions has not – a point stressed by all three authors. The recent Women into Public Life Campaign helped to focus public attention on the issue, and secured a commitment from the present Government, which Mary Baker records, to ensure the appointment of more women to public bodies. Jennifer Corcoran and Joni Lovenduski indicate in their report 'Women in Decisional Arenas in the UK' (Part 4 of a background report submitted to the EEC for use by European MPs in 1983) that women fare badly under governments of any hue, and that, at a local level, the Conservative Party has a better record than Labour.

Likewise, although women's membership of trades unions increased from 25 per cent in 1977 to 31 per cent in 1981, women still form a pathetically low proportion of trades union executives and full-time officials, as well as TUC delegates. In 1985, the National Union of Tailors and Garment Workers, with a 92.7 per cent female membership, had only seven women executive members out of a total of fourteen, three out of thirty-eight full-time officials, and sent only four women out of twelve delegates to the TUC. The National Union of Teachers, with 72.2 per cent women members, had only six women out of forty-seven executive members, two out of twenty-seven full-time officials, and three out of twenty-seven TUC delegates.

It should be added that there is virtually no evidence at all about the status of women amongst employers, including from those which proudly assert that they are 'equal opportunity employers'. In 1985 there were only two women on the 400-strong CBI General Council and only sixty-five women (out of a total of 3025) serving on the CBI's various committees. Although the CBI issued a model equal opportunity programme to all its members in 1979, in the wake of the Sex Discrimination Act, no monitoring of its implications has as yet taken place. Indeed, the CBI, with other pressure groups, was instrumental in gaining exemption for employers of five or fewer people from the Sex Discrimination Act, twenty or fewer from the Employment Act maternity provisions of 1980, and twenty or fewer in the unfair dismissal provisions of the Employment Protection (Consolidation) Act, unless the employee had worked for two years or more. The European Court has ruled against Britain in all these areas, and so the law has to be changed – to the enormous gratification of many women, no doubt, and not a few men.

The Europeans have a quite different attitude to legislation to protect women and the making of special provisions for women from that current in the USA and, to some extent, in Britain. The debate about competing 'equally' in the market simply does not apply, and there is a recognition of childcare as an important item on the political agenda. Within the EEC, France has arguably the best childcare provisions: there is a nationwide system of day nurseries and care for children below nursery age in crêches is the norm.

Outside the EEC, but deeply influential upon it, is Sweden, with its excellent parental leave provisions dating back in concept to the beginning of the century, its employment of people to care for sick children at home so that parents can continue to go to work (paid for on a means-tested basis), maternity leave on occasion up to two years in length, and excellent nursery provision. The argument about women returning home after the war and leaving the jobs to the men whilst they indulged in domestic bliss never took place in Scandinavia. The idea that domesticity itself was the acme of achievement and that a mother's role was to stimulate her baby from its earliest years did not hit the Europe of the 1950s as it did the USA and, by extension, Britain. Catholic Southern Europe saw children as an asset. Northern Europeans saw women as an asset in the workforce, not to be returned to their homes after the war. These were major differences, which had far-reaching effects once Britain entered the EEC.

The relationship with Europe is a crucial one in the debate about women's rights and the Conservatives have been less than keen on some of the measures proposed by the European Community to protect women. This was particularly the case with the EEC draft directive on part-time work, published in 1981. Eighty-four per cent of part-time workers in the UK are female, and there has been considerable growth in the availability of part-time work over recent years. The British Government has blocked that directive within the Council of Ministers on the basis that its provisions would discourage employers and so lead to the disappearance of even this valuable part-time work. Norman Tebbit argued in his submission to the House of Lords select committee on European legislation 'for sound commercial and economic reasons' against the directive, saying that any disadvantages that part-time workers suffered – if there were any – were 'a fact that part-time workers are ready to accept'.

Britain has also blocked the draft directives on parental leave and on temporary work, both of which are supported by Labour and the Alliance. Indeed there is a real argument of principle here, being voiced by some Conservatives, that the more employment protection provided for women, the fewer jobs will be available to them, simply because they will be decreasingly attractive to employers on the grounds of cost. Obviously the debate as to whether to legislate or let the market find its own level is a much broader one than the single issue of women's employment protection.

Sylvia Ann Hewlett criticised the American women's movement for concentrating too much on abortion and employment, and insufficiently on childcare and support for working women. All three contributors in this volume feel strongly that public policy should support women's choices, be those choices to work or to stay at home, and that adequate childcare provision should be made. The Alliance promises a year of pre-school education of some kind to all under-fives who want it. The Labour Party promises two years. Mary Baker argues that the Conservatives have already achieved a considerable amount with 47 per cent of all three- and four-year-olds in nursery and primary schools in 1985, compared with 35 per cent in 1976.

In many ways the women's debate has changed over the years. The belief in legislation, among some women at least, is waning, now that it looks as if it has not been as effective as they had hoped. The questions about whether the legislation was correctly framed or strong enough, whether the enforcement agency, the Equal Opportunities Commission, praised in one way or another by all three of our contributors, has sufficiently strong teeth, and about the extent to which there was ever serious intention amongst all the various groups involved to make the legislation work, are all too rarely addressed. Both Jane Ewart-Biggs and Mary Stott argue for more legislation to protect women's employment, mostly on the European model, and Mary Baker praises the work of the EOC, particularly in its campaigns to get more girls into science and engineering. Yet several writers have expressed their doubts, most notably, perhaps, Frances Cairncross in an article entitled 'Is the EOC worth £3 million of public money?'*

She argued that 'When the Commission was devised . . . it was designed with several serious built-in weaknesses. For instance, of the twelve Commissioners, three were to be appointed to represent the TUC and three the CBI. This was, from the first, a recipe for deadlock – or at least for an unholy alliance of employees and employers to prevent radical change . . .' She also asked whether it was possible for a Government-

---

* The *Guardian*, 7 December 1983.

funded watchdog to appoint effective critics of the status quo and criticised its record in conducting so very few formal investigations over its history. Yet its record has been good in criticising the Government over the vexed equal pay for work of equal value legislation. This was finally passed as the Equal Pay (Amendment) Act 1983 after much anger over the way the legislation was framed, with its 'tortuosity and complexity', as described by Lord Denning.* It also conducts excellent research, is a source of accurate and up-to-date information, and backs some cases in the Industrial Tribunal if it thinks they are good 'test' cases, where no other funding is available.

One of the questions which needs to be asked is whether any other agency could act better, whether some of the in-built weaknesses can be removed, and whether the idea of a Government-funded enforcement agency is doomed to failure in any case. One argument often used is that though governments of all complexions condemn discrimination and bring in measures designed to tackle it, such as the Sex Discrimination Act or the Equal Pay Act, and even set up enforcement agencies such as the EOC, they actually spend huge sums of money with firms or businesses which perpetuate the inequalities. This has led a considerable number of equal opportunities experts in Britain to argue that a contracts compliance policy should be entered into for the benefit of women, the disabled and ethnic minority groups. The Labour Party supports this idea, and the Alliance, too, is suggesting that, in government, it would only grant public contracts to employers who adopt and adhere to equal opportunities policies. To achieve equal opportunity status, an employer would have to submit its equal employment policy to the Human Rights Commission (which would contain amongst its other roles the functions of the old EOC), and submit to monitoring by it. This is the method used by the Americans with considerable success, and both the Labour Party and the

---

* Quoted in *Equal Value in Personnel Management* by David Wainwright (August 1986).

Alliance regard it as worth trying in the UK.

Employment is only one part of a woman's life, however. All the contributors to this volume address other issues, such as childcare, poverty, legal provisions and health. There is considerable evidence to suggest that the debate is moving away quite strongly from the legal enforcement approach to women's equality towards a greater emphasis on coping with special needs, on the European model. These range from specific provisions for women with children, such as workplace nurseries (which the Conservatives want to tax as a 'perk' although Mary Baker argues that the Conservative Women's National Committee is resisting strongly) to provisions for widows, supplementary benefit (when many single mothers with children live in poverty) and educational policies.

All three contributors are certain that equality for women is by no means won. Mary Baker is particularly concerned that barriers need to come down before there is any real sense of equality. 'We believe in open doors; many that were once barred to women are now plainly open, but some, though unlocked, still need a good shove to demonstrate to our daughters that women do have a vast range of futures waiting for them . . .' and 'Only when all the barriers are down can men and women play a full and equal part, with mutual respect and support, at work, in the community, and in the home.' She is ostensibly giving a Conservative point of view, which many 1960s feminists would have rejected out of hand. And yet the debate has come full circle, and most of the 'social feminists' of the 1980s would share her view to a very large extent.

The doubts arise with consideration of how to achieve that end. Is it enforcement that is needed? Or carrots? Or sticks and carrots? Is vast expenditure necessary to lift single-parent families, mostly headed by women, out of poverty? Or will stern economic medicine and the reduction of taxes create better opportunities for all, including those at the bottom of the pile? Can governments take action to ensure the promotion of women as role models for girls? Or should it be left to private individuals and companies? Is European legislation of benefit to British women? Or do some of its provisions act as a disincentive to many employers, making women too expensive to employ at all?

The issues addressed by our authors may be similar, but their methods of solving the problems posed differ considerably. They also differ enormously from other areas of the feminist debate. They are all liberal feminists (or social feminists) to a greater or lesser extent, in their belief that women's inequality can be largely rectified under the present system by legislation and education. They may differ as to the extent to which they believe that this is possible and, indeed, in how much they would be prepared to spend on it, but in principle they share this approach.

There are, however, two other main groups of feminist thinkers of greater or lesser significance: the 'socialist feminists' and the 'radical feminists'. The first, sometimes found on the edges of the Labour Party but mostly to the left of it, are those who believe that women's oppression can only end with the demise of the capitalist system. Until then it is legitimate to make demands of the state, providing it is always recognised that the state comprises both male and class power. Socialist feminists tend to become involved in specific campaigns about matters of concern to women – notably childcare, unlike the US, and women's working conditions, as well as cuts in various forms of benefit particularly likely to affect women. But they are always ambivalent about their role in 'male-defined' politics.

Radical feminists, on the other hand, believe that the fight is against institutionalised male power in all its forms. Men as a group benefit from the exploitation and oppression of women as a group. Change is only possible through women's collective action, and key issues are male violence, pornography, sexuality and the building of a women's culture. They do not regard it as essential (some not even as advisable) to draw men into supporting the feminist cause.

Obviously, this is a gross oversimplification of the situation, and many women who are feminists would not recognise themselves in any of these groups. Yet all three have had a remarkable effect on the political agenda in the UK. No politician would now dare dismiss women's issues and no party would be without a policy for women. The women's vote is valued and the role of women in public life is seen by all parties as an important area for examination. There are all-party attempts to get women on to public bodies, frequent, although often not very successful, attempts to get women appointed as directors of large companies and a recognition that the influence of role models is vital. Mary Baker puts it clearly: 'Every time we see a doctor who is a woman, a professor, an MP or a councillor, a camera operator or a judge, all women, and *all there on merit* (my underlining), it helps erode the still too prevalent concept that such jobs are really for men . . .'

The problem is how to define merit in a system where many of the top jobs are partly acquired through old boys' networks and the male environment of clubs and the Inns of Court. Mary Stott addresses the issue by saying that there is a need for positive discrimination (or affirmative action as it is now often described), and suggests that: 'It is often thought that positive discrimination leads to tokenism, and that to prefer the token woman, just because she is a woman, to an experienced and able man, is obviously undesirable as well as unfair. Yet for generations men have excluded women from all kinds of jobs on account of their sex, and I cannot bring myself to believe that if one woman here or there is not quite up to the job, she is inevitably worse than *any* of her male colleagues on the committee or board!'

Jane Ewart-Biggs takes up the same point in her insistence that more women be appointed to public bodies: 'The objective would not be to appoint women on to these bodies purely because they are women, with no regard to ability, but the Labour Party believes that there is a great number of women both able and willing to make a contribution to the work of these public bodies whilst at the same time occupying places to oversee other women's interests.'

All three contributions make much of the issue of women in public life. Yet there were no applications from women among the recent shortlisting for the new Director-General of the BBC. Similarly, when Professor Brenda Ryman, Mistress of Girton College, Cambridge, retired from her Chair at the Charing Cross Hospital a few years ago, no woman, out of over two hundred candidates, applied for her job. There is undeniably a problem for women putting themselves forward in Britain, and perhaps a further problem in that they are less likely to be 'invited to apply', given that they have no part in the old boys' network. Indeed, that is the argument most frequently used to encourage networking among women.

Public bodies are only one aspect of the issue, however. There are educational needs for women and girls, too, and housing needs, as graphically illustrated by Jane Ewart-Biggs. There is economic need and health need. There are questions to be asked about the current AIDS campaign and the spending on it in the face of 12,000 women dying every year from breast cancer of whom a quarter might be saved if there were screening facilities generally available to all. There are similar worries about the lack of adequate screening for cervical cancer, when early detection could save almost all the women affected. There are children's needs and needs for help in childcare. There are carers' needs as outlined by Mary Stott as more and more women end up looking after their elderly and disabled relatives at home. There are legal needs, such as those for a family court rather than the adversarial system of the present divorce proceedings. And there is a need for a national conciliation service to minimise the appalling effects of marital break-up on the adults concerned, but, even more, on the children.

In recognising these needs, all three contributors are influenced by the thinking of the 1960s. To some extent, they were part of it. And yet, though in the 1960s and 1970s feminist thinking and sexual politics entered the political arena, very little progress towards equality has been achieved. Few major changes have occurred in most women's lives. The wage gap is widening, and Julie Hayward has just lost her case for equal pay for equal value, on the argument that her fringe benefits are better than any man's with whom she was comparing herself – yet she would need to take something like thirteen weeks a year in sick leave in order for that to be financially true. This decision will put back the progress of cases claiming equal pay for equal value quite considerably, since the grounds on which equal value can be claimed will be much narrowed. But this is typical of a period when progress for women seems to be declining in the measurable areas such as pay, position, promotion and employment protection.

Many women, particularly those who head single-parent families, live in poverty. Backlash debates still occur, as evidenced by the Church of England's argument on the ordination of women. There are still few role models. Consciousness-raising may even have made matters worse by turning the issue to the inside, rather than encouraging campaigning in the outside world. The American model is still prevalent in Britain, and there is still reluctance to see ourselves as 'Europeans' with a recognition of women's special needs.

The challenge for the late 1980s and 1990s is about how these needs are to be met. Is the answer to make sure that women have more money, so that they can make their own choices? Those who advocate major tax changes think that women being in charge of their own financial affairs would be of great benefit. It is by campaigning for equal pay, and fighting the 'equal pay for work of equal value' cases as they come up? Is it by having benefits paid directly to the caring parent so that it cannot be drunk away? Or is it by increasing cash benefits, as Labour and the Alliance want to do, but also keeping benefits in kind where appropriate? If we encourage people to make their own choices, how do we help them when they have made the wrong one, or when their dependants suffer as a result? Is it the enabling state that we want, or the nanny state, or is it a kindly aunt in between who will not interfere, but will occasionally pick up the pieces?

These are all issues of crucial importance to women, and the answers are by no means clear. We have moved a long way from 'Sisterhood is powerful'. Recognition of the part women have to play in society as it is structured has now been achieved, as has an awareness that it is not yet easy for women to reach the positions where they can play that part. Tackling this problem is, perhaps, the next item on the political agenda.